YASHA BERESINER

Lewis Masonic

First published 2012

ISBN 978 0 85318 413 3

Published by Lewis Masonic

an imprint of Ian Allan Publishing Ltd, Hersham, Surrey KT12 4RG.
Printed in England by Ian Allan Printing Ltd, Hersham, Surrey KT12 4RG.

Visit the Lewis Masonic website at
www.lewismasonic.co.uk

'Anecdotes and maxims are rich treasures to the man of the world, for he knows how to introduce the former at fit place in conversation.'
Johann Wolfgang von Goethe (1749-1832)

'It is good for an uneducated man to read books of quotations.'
Winston Churchill (1874-1965)

'It is better to be quotable than to be honest.'
Tom Stoppard (1937-)

'I often quote myself… it adds spice to my conversation.'
George Bernard Shaw (1856-1950)

'A proverb is one man's wit and all men's wisdom.'
Lord John Russell (1792-1878)

'The wisdom of the wise and the experience of the ages may be preserved by quotations.'
Benjamin Disraeli (1804-1881)

Contents

Dedication

This little booklet is dedicated with love and in long standing friendship, to my one and only brother, Jos.

Foreword

METROPOLITAN GRAND LODGE
of
LONDON

R W Bro Russell J Race, JP, DL
Metropolitan Grand Master

Autumn 2012

Dear Reader,

The success of Freemasonry through the ages has been brought about by that fine balance between seriousness and fun reflected in the dignity of our ceremonies and the humour we so often enjoy in our after proceedings. This little booklet, compiled by Yasha Beresiner, reflects that humour that is such an essential ingredient in Masonic harmony.

Yasha, a London Mason, is well known in our Metropolitan Grand Lodge and, indeed, throughout the Masonic community here and abroad. He lectures extensively and many Brethren will have enjoyed his after dinner speeches. This booklet will assist in disseminating his special brand of humour and I am very pleased to recommend it to you all to assist you with your own after dinner efforts.

Wishing you all Happy Freemasonry

Russell Race

Acknowledgements

My thanks are extended to numerous individuals and Brethren who have continuously provided me with material, anecdotes and stories: my darling daughter Dana has been a constant and consistent source, especially with truths uttered by my wonderful grandchildren, Dassi, Tali, Michal and Shira. (Seven-year-old Shira's latest quotable statement on being told that a TV programme, which she had previously watched with her older sisters, was not suitable for her age, was: *'I used to watch that programme but now I am too young!'*). The indefatigable Martin Faulks is a special colleague and guide; Ronnie San, Issa Tahan and Lance Whitehouse are great story-tellers and excellent friends, as is Sheila Evered, who again proof read the manuscript for me. There are many who have assisted me without even being aware of it. As is now customary, I have used many internet sources, here generally acknowledged. I have made liberal use of AQC, the transactions of Quatuor Coronati Lodge No. 2076 and have listed in the bibliography other additional and specific sources used.

About the author

Yasha Beresiner was born in Turkey in 1940 and is a Law Graduate of the Hebrew University of Jerusalem. He moved to England in 1969 and after an extended career as a legal consultant was appointed a Director of Stanley Gibbons Ltd, the stamp magnates. In 1983 he set up his own company InterCol London (www.intercol.co.uk). He is a City of London Guide (Editor of their quarterly publication) and a Past Master of the Worshipful Company of Makers of Playing Cards, founded in 1628. He is a lecturer and the author of a dozen books, including five on Freemasonry, and many articles in various specialised publications throughout Europe and the Americas. He was initiated in London in 1975 and in 1992 he was invited to become a full member of the Quatuor Coronati Lodge No. 2076, the Premier Lodge of Masonic Research, serving as Master in 1998/9.

By the same author

The Paper Tiger, (with Art Buchwald & Uri Ben-Yehuda),
    Eichenberger 1968
Colombian Currency, Stanley Gibbons 1973
The Story of Paper Money, (with C Narbeth),
    David & Charles 1974
A Collectors' Guide to Paper Money, Andre Deutsch, 1977
British County Maps, ACC 1983
The Ortiz-Patiño Collection of Playing Cards, InterCol 1995
Masonic Curiosities, ANZMRC 1999
Royal Arch: the 4th degree of the Antients,
    Supreme Grand Chapter of England 2000
City of London - a Masonic Guide,
    Lewis Masonic 2007, (reprinted 2011)
Masonically Speaking, Lewis Masonic 2008
Freemasons' Handbook of Toasts, Speeches and Responses,
    Lewis Masonic 2009

Bibliography

Breverton, Terry *Immortal Last Words* London 2010
Cagney, Peter *Book of Wit & Humour* A Thomas 1976
Foster, W & Bryant H *Comprehension and Composition*,
    Sydney, Australia
Hamill, John & Gilbert, Robert (Ed) *Freemasonry – A
    Celebration of the Craft* London 1998
http://rhetoric.byu.edu
http://www.awordinyoureye.com
http://www.quotesandsayings.com
Klein, Shelley *The Book of Senior Moments* London 2006
Morris, Brent S *The Complete Idiot's Guide to Freemasonry*
    Penguin (USA) 2006
Power, George *A Masonic Collection* Privately printed Antrim
    1989

Prochnow, Herbert V *The Public Speaker's Treasure Chest*
Northampton 1954
(1st Edition)
Robertson, Bengt (Ed) *The Wordsworth Book of Quotations* 2011
Sherrin, Ned (Ed) *The Oxford Dictionary of Humorous Quotations* Oxford 2008
Zeldis, Leon *Quips, Squibs and Some Quotations* New Orleans 2008

Introduction

Paul Johnson (1928-), the eminent journalist and author, is of the opinion that the earliest joke ever – about 2000BC – was female and was about sex. He uses a quote from the Old Testament as evidence that it was a woman who first laughed:

> '…and Sarah his wife shall have a son. And Sarah heard it in the tent door, which was behind him…Therefore Sarah laughed within herself, saying, After I am waxed old shall I have pleasure, my Lord being old also?'
> (Genesis 18. 10/12)

I feel, therefore, I am following a very long tradition with this booklet. It consists mainly of quotations, with a few anecdotes, poems and rhymes, added as seasoning, so to speak. These are derived from every conceivable source. The bibliographic listing, as extensive as it could have been, would not have done justice to all the available sources used: other literature comprising books, transactions, magazines, etc., the media, personal utterances and, of course, the internet. Since there is no such thing as copyright on quotations, I have avoided attributions in the main body of the book. I may even be guilty of misquotations. Nonetheless, the reader will undoubtedly recognise some immortal quotes. Others are from less famous personalities, some infamous ones and other unknown authors, including myself. I have in mind, you see, what Jean de la Bruyère (1645-1696), the French essayist and moralist, commented 350 years ago:

> 'A man often runs the risk of throwing away a witticism if he admits that it is his own.'

Naturally Part 3 devoted to sayings by famous Freemasons (or famous men who happened to also be Freemasons) has the correct attributions. So does the Appendix where sayings, transliterated into English, are dedicated to global proverbs. I can, therefore, more accurately describe myself as the compiler of this small tome, rather than its author. This booklet is meant to be practical, not just amusing but also 'clever', with a touch of those well-known philosophies we so readily recognise as true to life. The editor of *The Oxford Dictionary of Quotations* stated:

'Ideally a quotation should be able to float free from its moorings, remaining detached from its original context.'

Should you be given just a few moments to prepare for a speech, you will readily be able to **locate**, within the pages of this book, a statement that will allow you to **enhance** any short comment you make, giving it immediate **relevance**. **Locate** by using the novel A to Z index tags; **enhance** by attributing an anecdote or quote to what you say; and **make relevant** by associating the subject to the evening's proceedings. It is for this reason that the content has been organised thematically except for the alphabetic listing of the sayings of famous Freemasons. In this Third Part, extended Masonic biographic notes have been included to add some depth to the comments that are made. Make good use of them. Remember not to add further comment when making a quote. A quote will stand on its own and an added comment, such as '*You know what I mean*' or '*Isn't that wise?*' etc., may well ruin the effect. By failing to prepare, you are preparing to fail!

The light-hearted quotes are invariably witticisms. Wit is intended to be fun as opposed to humour that is funny. A subtle but important difference for after dinner speakers. Witticism will often generate a smile and light laughter, as is intended in the dignified surroundings of a festive board held in a stately dining room. This is in contrast to the humour of a stand-up comic who generates loud and noisy laughter. An after dinner speaker is not a stand-up comedian and is not expected to rattle off a series of jokes and anecdotes unrelated to each other. An after dinner speaker has body and a theme to his speech and his anecdotes and quotes are linked and emphasise aspects of what he is saying. This is also a good opportunity to mention, with as much weight as possible, the importance of brevity. A brief speech will allow your words to be absorbed and retained. Brevity will guarantee the success of your speech.

This book follows on from my two earlier publications by Lewis Masonic, namely *Masonically Speaking* and *Freemasons' Handbook of Toasts, Speeches and Responses*. The former in particular will prove helpful in general directives about after dinner speaking. Space does not allow for the repetition of the many guidelines given there. Whilst I can repeat that there is no such thing as a new story – only whether you have heard it before or not – there is, in fact, no repetition of text or anecdotes from my earlier publications in this booklet. Not that repetition is prohibitive. A good story well told is as amusing when repeated as it was when first told. It is, however, important to keep away from, or at least be very careful and delicate with sensitive subjects such as death, sex and race. When selecting the quotes below, I remained constantly aware of these sensibilities. Although I have included three quotes under the heading of 'No-no', in general I have kept away from sex, race and cruelty, as well as from impossible circumstances, such as talking animals, heaven and earth, etc. Clearly several quotes could be under different headings and there is no particular rhyme or reason to my selection of a specific heading.

The selection of quotes was dictated by some relevance, direct or indirect, to social functions, activities and temperament, with Freemasonry in mind. Using just three quotes for any subject was dictated by the size of this booklet. The quotes attributed to famous Masons are, so far as can be ascertained, all genuine. A good quote is one with which your listeners can immediately identify. In this context, when asked to speak, listen carefully to what is being said by others and keep your eyes and mind open to your surroundings as anything could be helpful with regard to relevance: a painting on the wall, unusual furniture or décor, members of the catering staff – all these subjects can be mentioned in your brief and impromptu speech. Remember, the more you are able to prepare, the more spontaneous your speech can appear to be! Make use of the themes and specific statements or known personalities of other speakers: insurance brokers, academics, musicians, etc. There is nothing that should stop you from personalising and adapting the wording of any quote to your own specific needs. I have used the simplest of names 'John' where this was relevant in a quote. You may easily replace the name with that of a person who will be readily recognised by your audience, such as the Chairman or another speaker. There are three key factors I would like to remind you of as a speaker, when making a quote (or speaking in general):

- Speak slowly, clearly and loudly
- Emphasise the punch line or key word
- Personalise where possible

The most important factor in giving a successful speech is timing. In order to guide the reader to the emphasis needed, in some quotes I have used three dots…to indicate emphasis. This is achieved by resounding silence before uttering the last few key words. It generates anticipation. A good example is: '*I pay my accountant to save me time…in prison*'. Here anything but perfect timing, i.e. a long pause before saying 'in prison', will spoil the effect of the anecdote. Careful timing will enhance it. Many of the quotes are a play on words and on most such occasions the quote itself will dictate its utterance, that is where the emphasis is to be placed. As a final note to this brief introduction, may I remind you to use '*who was it that said …*' liberally, unless, of course, you can identify the author of the quote or you are confident enough to know that no one else in your audience would know anyway.

Part 1

Wordplay

The intricate wonders of the English language are manifest in these quotations. I considered it, therefore, appropriate to give a brief review, with examples, of what is wordplay, as used in the following pages. As this book is essentially a compilation of quotes, it is worthwhile to briefly consider the literary technique used by so many talented authors. The basic concept of wordplay is that the words themselves used in the quote are the subject of the work. This is intended specifically to amuse. The various forms that such wordplay takes are described below. Studying examples of wordplay is not only entertaining and often humorous, but it also allows you, as a speaker, to note how language is at work and apply your own more elaborate and sophisticated techniques as you grow more confident with greater experience. Here are some simplistic definitions and examples of the most common expressions used throughout literature by well-known and unknown authors.

You may like to try your hand at creating your own wordplay using the defined criteria.

ADAGE
The word has been in use since the 1540s and is derived from the Latin adagium: 'to speak'. An adage is used in order to convey a traditional saying accepted to be true, based on life experience:

* *Do not count your chickens before they are hatched.*
* *Don't burn bridges behind you.*
* *Pardon the expression.*

ANAGRAM

Used as early as 1580, the origin of the word is from the Greek words *ana* = 'back' and *gramma* = 'letter', thus 'transpose letters'. An anagram reproduces exactly the same letters in a word or sentence but in a different order. Thus an anagram rearranges all of the original letters in order to create a new word or phrase:

* *The nudist colony: no untidy clothes.*
* *Animosity — is no amity.*
* *A decimal point — I'm a dot in place.*

APHORISM

The literal translation of the word from the Greek, where the term was first used in the 4th century BC, is: 'distinction' or 'definition'. An aphorism is a brief and succinct statement of an original true or cleverly expressed thought. The use of aphorisms has been called Wisdom Literature and has been used by many clever and famous individuals. Here are three examples by three celebrities:

* *As far as the laws of mathematics refer to reality, they are not certain, and as far as they are certain, they do not refer to reality.* (Albert Einstein)
* *The best argument against democracy is a five-minute conversation with the average voter.* (Winston Churchill)
* *Death is one of the few things that can be done as easily lying down. The difference between sex and death is that with death you can do it alone and no-one is going to make fun of you. (*Woody Allen*)*

CHARADE

Charade is a word derived from the French for entertainment and can be traced back to the mid-18th century. In wordplay a charade is achieved when two different sentences are incorporated in a brief statement of single words. This is particularly useful for after dinner speaking as often the best effect of a charade is expressed aloud:

* *He knowingly led and we blindly followed.*
* *By day the frolic, and the dance by night.*
* *Amiable together…am I able to get her?*

CHIASMUS

A chiasmus, from the Greek *chiasmós* meaning 'equivalent to', is where an idea is repeated in inverted order. The technique has been in literary use for a hundred and fifty years. The best known and most familiar example is the first one given below by John Kennedy at his inaugural address on 20 January 1961:

* *Ask not what your country can do for you — ask what you can do for your country.*
* *It is boring to eat; to sleep is fulfilling.*
* *I'd rather have a bottle in front of me than a frontal lobotomy.*

CLICHÉ

The French origin of the word, dating to the 1830s, is interesting. It refers to the printing process, the stereotype plate and the 'click' sound caused by the metal being pressed against the matrix. A cliché is an expression, true or not, that has lost its original meaning due to overuse. It is all the more effective when in its original form it was meaningful. Be careful using clichés in your speech as they have a tendency to sound false.

* *Finding your way and keeping the faith.*
* *Misery loves company.*
* *You can catch more flies with honey than with vinegar.*

OXYMORON

An oxymoron, where an adjective contradicts a noun, is derived from the Greek meaning 'foolish' or 'stupid' and dates to 1657. It is also known as 'contradiction', which explains the term very well. An oxymoron familiar to Freemasons, given as the first example, is the title of Walton Hannah's well-known exposure first published in 1952:

* *Darkness visible.*
* Loud silence.
* Deep down I think that I am pretty superficial.

PALINDROME

A palindrome is another old expression from the early 17th century derived from the Greek *palíndromos* 'running back again' or 'recurring'. In a palindrome the word or sentence reads the same whether read forwards or backwards.

* *Madam, I'm Adam.*
* *A man, a plan, a canal — Panama.*
* *King…are you glad you are King?*

PARADOX

A paradox has been well described as being to the written word what an optical illusion is to the eye. It consists of a logical thought leading to a contradiction in terms defying the logic. It is a contradiction emanating from circular thinking. Socrates, quoted as the first example, may well have been the first to use a paradox, in the 5th century BC:

* *As for me, all I know is that I know nothing.*
* *If there is an exception to every rule, then every rule must have at least one exception; the exception to this one being that it has no exception.*
* *This booklet will undoubtedly be found interesting by those who take an interest in it.*

PROVERB

A proverb is a popular saying of unknown origin that is truthful and universally familiar, simply expressed. Its origin is Middle English used as early as the 13th century. It is synonymous with many of the wordplay examples given here. Every culture has proverbs of its own (see Appendix).

* *Haste makes waste.*
* *You can lead a horse to water, but you can't make him drink.*
* *Those who live in glass houses shouldn't throw stones.*

PUN

In simple terms a pun is a humorous play on words. The word is possibly derived from the Italian *punctilio* for word-play, or is, more likely, of mid-17th century English origin, A pun is often at the expense of another but not intended to be serious or offensive. It will frequently incorporate ambiguities.

* *Ben Battle was a soldier bold, and used to war's alarms:*
  But a cannonball took off his legs, so he laid down his arms.
* *A man who could make so vile a pun would not scruple to pick a pocket.*
* *A pun is a punishable offence.*

SPOONERISM

A spoonerism is the spontaneous inclination to mix up words (or wix up murds). The idea was invented by the Reverend William Archibald Spooner (1844-1930), Warden of New College, Oxford, who is credited with much more than he ever uttered. The term *spoonerism* has been in use since 1885. Well-known actors and comedians have created whole poems and stories using spoonerisms. Here are three examples of spoonerisms attributed to Spooner himself:

* *The weight of rages will press hard upon the employer.*
  (rate of wages)
* *Three cheers for our queer old dean.* (dear old queen)
* *You hissed my mystery lecture.* (missed my history lecture)

Spooner also acted out his ideas: it is reported he once spilled salt at a dinner and carefully poured some wine on it. He also once remarked of a widow that *'her husband was eaten by missionaries'*.

Part 2

An ABC of Quotes and Anecdotes

Accountants

* *When I asked my accountant if anything could get me out of this mess I am in now, he thought for a long time and said, 'Yes, death would help.'*
* *My accountant has advised me to spend a year dead...for tax reasons.*
* *Over the long haul of life on this planet, it is the ecologists, and not the bookkeepers of business, who are the ultimate accountants.*

Acting

* *A good actor must never be distracted by love...except for himself.*
* *Acting consists of the ability to stop your audience from coughing.*
* *On stage he was natural, simple, affecting; it was only off stage that he was acting.*

Action

* *Nothing is impossible for the person who does not have to do it.*
* *In any given set of circumstances, the proper course of action is determined by subsequent events.*
* *A man of words and not of deeds, like a garden full of weeds.*

Advertising

* *Advertising is the science of arresting human intelligence long enough to get money from it.*
* *The consumer is not a moron...she is your wife.*

*   *I think that I shall never see*
    A billboard lovely as a tree;
    Perhaps, unless the billboards fall,
    I'll never see a tree at all.

Advice

*   *I always advise youngsters never to use the word 'always'.*
*   *Sound advice is ninety-nine per cent sound and one per cent advice*
*   *The best time to give advice to your children is while they're still young enough to believe you know what you're talking about.*

Age

*   *Growing old is mandatory – but growing up…that is optional.*
*   *Growing old is not nice… but it is interesting.*
*   *A man of sixty has spent twenty years in bed and over three years in eating.*

Alcohol

*   *An alcoholic is any man you do not like…that drinks as much as you do.*
*   *Alcohol does not solve any problems, but then again neither does milk.*
*   *The innkeeper loves the drunkard, but not for a son-in-law.*

America

*   *America is a vast conspiracy to make you happy.*
*   *Never criticise Americans…they have the best taste that money can buy.*
*   *To Americans, English manners are far more frightening than no manners at all.*

Anger

*   *Anger rusts the heart.*

* When angry, count to four; when very angry…swear.
* Those who in quarrels interpose,
  Most often wipe a bloody nose.

Architecture
* The physician can bury his mistakes, but the architect can only advise his client to plant vines.
* The Pavilion
  Cost a million
  As a monument to Art,
  And the wits here
  Say it sits here
  Like an Oriental tart!
* Ghastly good taste – or a depressing story of the rise and fall of English architecture.

Argument
* If you cannot answer a man's argument, all is not lost…you can still call him vile names.
* It is a sad thing that people can only agree about what they are not really interested in.
* 'Shut up,' he explained.

Atheism
* 'As an atheist, what will you say when you die and you are brought face to face with your Maker?'
  'God,' I will say … 'God, why did you make the evidence for your existence so insufficient?'
* An atheist is a man who has no invisible means of support.
* Thank God I am still an atheist.

Bachelor
* A bachelor never makes the same mistake once.

*   *She was another one of his near Mrs.*
*   *A bachelor's life is no life for a single man.*

Banks
*   *It has become so bad that if the bank returns your cheque marked 'Insufficient Funds' you have to call them and ask if they mean you or them.*
*   *A bank's policy is that you must never lend any money to anybody unless they don't need it*
*   *In '29 when banks went bust –*
    Our coins still read 'In God We Trust'…(Everyone else, pay cash.)

Beauty
*   *Manners are especially the need of the plain. The pretty can get away with anything.*
*   *She has eyes that men adore so, and a torso…even more so.*
*   *Beauty is only sin deep.*

Begging
*   *As for begging, it is safer to beg than to take, but it is finer to take than to beg.*
*   *Gentility without ability is worse than plain beggary.*
*   *Beggars should be abolished: it is annoying to give to them and it is annoying not to give to them.*

Bigamy
*   *Bigamy is having one wife too many. Monogamy…is the same.*
*   *Bigamy is the only crime where two rights make a wrong.*
*   *It wouldn't make much sense to increase the penalty for bigamy. A bigamist has two mothers-in-law, and that's punishment enough.*

Birth
*   *To my embarrassment I was born in bed with a lady.*

* *Your birth is a mistake you'll spend your whole life trying to correct.*
* *Birth and death are not two different states, but they are different aspects of the same. There is as little reason to deplore the one as there is to be pleased over the other.*

Books
* *This is not a novel to be tossed aside lightly…it should be thrown with great force.*
* *I read part of the book all the way through.*
* *Should not the Society of Indexers be known as Indexers, Society of, The?*

Bores
* *A bore is someone who talks when you want him to listen.*
* *A bore is a man who, when you ask him how he is, tells you.*
* *He was not only a bore…he bored for England.*

Boxing
* *To me, boxing is like a ballet, except there's no music, no choreography, and the dancers hit each other.*
* *Boxing is a celebration of the lost religion of masculinity, all the more trenchant for its being lost.*
* *The third man in the ring makes boxing possible.*

Britain
* *Freedom of the press in Britain is freedom to print such of the proprietor's prejudices as the advertisers won't object to.*
* *In the end it may well be that Britain will be honoured by historians more for the way she disposed of an empire than for the way in which she acquired it.*
* *The British public has always had an unerring taste for ungifted amateurs.*

Bureaucracy

* *Join in the new game that's sweeping the country. It's called 'Bureaucracy'.*
  Everybody stands in a circle. The first person to do anything loses.
* *The only thing that saves us from the bureaucracy is its inefficiency.*
* *Bureaucracy is the art of making the possible impossible.*

Business

* *I have made it a rule of my life to make business a pleasure... and pleasure my business.*
* *A budget tells us what we can't afford, but it doesn't keep us from buying it.*
* *Business, that's easily defined – it is other people's money.*
  Charity
* *It is more agreeable to have the power to give than to receive.*
* *If there be any truer measure of a man by what he does, it must be by what he gives.*
* *We are rich only through what we give; and poor only through what we refuse and keep.*

Charm

* *Charm is the way of getting the answer 'Yes' without having asked the question.*
* *Modesty: the gentle art of enhancing your charm by pretending not to be aware of it.*
* *It is absurd to divide people into good and bad. People are either charming or tedious.*

Children

* *Children have never been very good at listening to their elders but they have never failed to imitate them.*

* *Children begin by loving their parents; as they grow older they judge them; sometimes they forgive them.*
* *Adults are always asking little kids what they want to be when they grow up because they're looking for ideas.*

Cleanliness
* *Take a bath…you're like the second week of a garbage strike.*
* *Cleanliness is almost as bad as godliness.*
* *Mrs. Joe was a very clean housekeeper, but had an exquisite art of making her cleanliness more uncomfortable and unacceptable than dirt itself.*

Comedy
* *Comedy is simply a funny way of being serious.*
* *The world is a comedy to those who think, a tragedy to those who feel.*
* *All comedies are ended by a marriage – all tragedies are finished by a death.*

Commandments
* *The seventh commandment is: 'Thou Shalt Not Admit Adultery' (Schoolboy)*
* *It is easier to keep holidays than commandments.*
* *'Thou shalt not get found out' is not one of God's commandments; and no man can be saved by trying to keep it.*

Committees
* *A committee is a group of people who can do nothing, but collectively meet and decide nothing can be done.*
* *A committee of one gets things done.*
* *'The members of the Committee wish you a speedy recovery – four in favour, two abstentions.'*

Compromise

* *A compromise is an agreement where both parties get what neither of them want.*

* *Compromise is the art of dividing a cake in such a way as to make everybody believe that they got the biggest slice.*

* *Compromise is but the sacrifice of one right or good in the hope of retaining another – too often ending in the loss of both.*

Computers

* *Where there is artificial intelligence…there must also be artificial stupidity.*

* *The perfect computer has been developed. You just feed in your problems and they never come out again.*

* *Programming today is a race between software engineers striving to build bigger and better idiot-proof programs and the universe trying to produce bigger and better idiots. So far, the universe is winning.*

Conversation

* *He had lost the art of conversation but not, unfortunately, the power of speech.*

* *Wit is the salt of conversations…not the food.*

* *There is no conversation more boring than the one where everybody agrees.*

Courage

* *Courage is what it takes to stand up and speak; courage is also what it takes to sit down and listen.*

* *It hurts to love someone and not be loved in return, but what is the most painful is to love someone and never find the courage to let the person know how you feel.*

* *A great leader's courage to fulfil his vision comes from passion, not position.*

Cricket

*   *The game explained:*
    You have two sides out in the field, and one is in.
    Each man that is in the side that is in gets called out, and when
    he is out he goes in, and the next man goes in, until he is out.
    When they are all out, the side that is out comes in, and the side
    that has been in goes out and tries to get those who are in, out.
    Sometimes you get men still in who are not out.
*   *Many Continentals think life is a game; the English think
    cricket is a game.*
*   *I tend to think that cricket is the greatest thing that God ever
    created on earth – certainly greater than sex, although sex isn't
    too bad either.*

Critics

*   *A critic is a man who knows the way but cannot drive the car.*
*   *It behoves every man to remember that the work of the critic is
    of altogether secondary importance, and that, in the end,
    progress is accomplished by the man who does things.*
*   *Whatever course you decide upon, there is always someone to tell
    you that you are wrong. There are always difficulties arising
    which tempt you to believe that your critics are right. To map
    out a course of action and follow it to an end requires courage.*

Dancing

*   *Do not try to dance better than anyone else. I only try to dance
    better than myself.*
*   *Dancing is the perpendicular expression of the horizontal desire.*
*   *Those who danced were thought to be quite insane by those who
    could not hear the music.*

Death

*   *I want to die like my granddad, peacefully in my sleep, not
    screaming…like the passengers on his bus.*

* Here am I, dying of a hundred good symptoms.
* When I die I'm going to leave my body to science fiction.

Democracy
* Democracy is government by discussion, but it is only effective if you can stop people talking.
* Democracy is being allowed to vote for the candidate you dislike least.
* We'd all like to vote for the best man but he's never a candidate.

Dignity
* I left the room in silent dignity, but caught my foot in the mat.
* What should move us to action is human dignity; the inalienable dignity of the oppressed, but also the dignity of each of us. We lose dignity if we tolerate the intolerable.
* Dignity does not consist in possessing honours, but in deserving them.

Diplomacy
* Diplomacy is telling someone to go to hell, so that they actually look forward to it.
* An ambassador is an honest man sent abroad to lie for the good of his country.
* Diplomacy is the art of letting someone have your way.

Divorce
* I'm an excellent housekeeper. Every time I get a divorce, I keep the house.
* Nowadays love is a matter of chance, matrimony a matter of money and divorce a matter of course.
* Divorce…from the Latin word meaning to rip out a man's genitals through his wallet.

Doctors

* *God heals and the doctor takes the fees.*
* *A doctor kills your ills with pills...and kills you with bills.*
* *My doctor gave me six months to live, but when I couldn't pay the bill he gave me six months more.*

Dogs

* *I am not a dog-lover – to me a dog-lover is a dog that is in love with another dog.*
* *A woman who is really kind to a dog is always one who has failed to inspire sympathy in men.*
* *A dog is the only thing on earth that loves you more than you love yourself.*

Dreams

* *Dream as if you'll live forever; live as if you'll die today.*
* *The best thing about dreams is that fleeting moment, when you are between asleep and awake, when you don't know the difference between reality and fantasy, when for just that one moment, you feel with your entire soul that the dream is reality, and it really happened.*
* *May the love hidden deep inside your heart find the love waiting in your dreams.*

May the laughter that you find in your tomorrow wipe away the pain you find in your yesterdays

Drink

* *Never drink on an empty stomach...make sure you have a couple of beers first.*
* *Work is the curse of the drinking classes.*
* *But I am not so think as you drunk I am.*

Eccentricity

* *Eccentricity, to be socially acceptable, has still to have at least four or five generations of inbreeding behind it.*
* *I am not eccentric. It's just that I am more alive than most people. I am an unpopular electric eel set in a pond of goldfish.*
* *When I was losing, they called me nuts. When I was winning they called me eccentric.*

Economics

* *It is a recession when your neighbour loses his job. It becomes a depression when you lose yours.*
* *An economist is an expert who will know tomorrow why the things he predicted yesterday didn't happen today.*
* *Save water…shower with a friend.*

Education

* *I didn't have any education. I had to use my brains.*
* *Education is what is left when you have forgotten all that you have learnt.*
* *Intelligence enables a man to get along in life without education and education enables him to get along in life without intelligence.*

Encouragement

* *When a man ain't got a rap, an' he's feelin' kind of blue,*
  An' the clouds hang dark an' heavy, an' won't let sunshine through,
  It's a great thing, O my brethren, for a feller just to lay
  His hand upon your shoulder in a friendly sort o' way.
  It makes a man feel curious; it makes the tear drops start,
  An' you sort o' feel a flutter in the region of the heart.
  You can't look up and meet his eyes; you don't know what to say
  When his hand is on your shoulder in a friendly sort o' way.
  Oh, the world's a curious compound, with its honey and its gall,
  With its cares and bitter crosses; but a good world after all.

An' a good God must have made it – leastways, that's what I say,
When a hand rests on my shoulder in a friendly sort o' way.
* *Every child should have an occasional pat on the back…as long as it is applied long enough and hard enough.*
* *Correction does much, but encouragement does more.*

Enemies
* *John doesn't have an enemy in the world, and none of his friends like him either.*
* *Love your enemies…it makes them so damned mad.*
* *He who has a thousand friends has not a friend to spare, and he who has one enemy will meet him everywhere.*

Enthusiasm
* *Success is going from failure to failure without losing enthusiasm.*
* *Enthusiasm is the mother of effort, and without it nothing great was ever achieved.*
* *It's enthusiasm for something and faith in something that makes a life worth living.*

Eternity
* *Eternity is a really terrible thought…I mean, where is it all going to end?*
* *Love is not written on paper, for paper can be erased. Nor is it etched on stone, for a stone can be broken. But it is inscribed on a heart and there it shall remain forever.*
* *Life has no meaning the moment you lose the illusion of being eternal.*

Exaggeration
* *There are some men so addicted to exaggeration that they cannot tell the truth without lying.*
* *An exaggeration is a truth that has lost its temper.*
* *Mysticism and exaggeration go together. A mystic must not fear ridicule if he is to push all the way to the limits of humility or the limits of delight.*

Experience

* *Experience is what you get when you don't get what you want.*
* *Experience is the name every one gives to their mistakes.*
* *Until this moment, I never understood how hard it was to lose something you never had.*

Experts

* *An expert is a man who tells you a simple thing in a confused way in such a fashion as to make you think the confusion is your own fault.*
* *An expert is someone who knows more and more about less and less, until eventually he knows everything about nothing.*
* *If an expert says it can't be done...get another expert.*

Failure

* *There is much to be said for failure. It is more interesting than success.*
* *That poor man...he is completely unspoiled by failure.*
* *If you are going to fail, you might as well do it trying the impossible.*

Faith

* *You don't have to be an angel in order to be a saint.*
* *Faith is much better than belief. Belief is when someone else does the thinking.*
* *I respect faith...but doubt is what educates you.*

Fame

* *It took me 15 years to discover that I had no talent for acting/writing but I couldn't give it up because by then I was too famous.*
* *All my life, I always wanted to be somebody. Now I see that I should have been more specific.*
* *Only great men may have great faults.*

Family
* *Absence is one of the most useful ingredients of family life and to do it rightly is an art like any other*
* *The families of one's friends are always a disappointment.*
* *One would be in less danger*
  From the wiles of a stranger
  If one's own kin and kith
  Were more fun to be with.

Fanatics
* *A fanatic is one who cannot change his mind and will not change the subject.*
* *The whole problem with the world is that fools and fanatics are always so certain of themselves, but wiser people are so full of doubts.*
* *Sexual love is undoubtedly one of the chief things in life, and the union of mental and bodily satisfaction in the enjoyment of love is one of its culminating peaks. Apart from a few queer fanatics, all the world knows this and conducts its life accordingly; science alone is too delicate to admit it.*

Fart
* *A fart is a breeze*
  That gives the stomach ease;
  It disinfects the bed-clothes
  And suffocates the fleas.
* *Love is the fart of every heart: it pains a man when it is kept close, and offends others when it is let loose.*
* *I'm a fart in a gale of wind, a humble violet, under a cow pat.*

Fathers
* *A father is a banker provided by nature.*
* *One night a father overheard his son pray: 'Dear God, make me the kind of man my daddy is'. Later that night, the father*

prayed: 'Dear God, make me the kind of man my son wants me to be.'

* *My father didn't tell me how to live; he lived, and let me watch him do it.*

Food

* *'What are you doing for dinner tonight?' – 'Digesting it!'*
* *He that lives upon hope will die fasting.*
* *I used to eat a lot of natural foods until I learned that most people die of natural causes.*

Football

* *Some people think football is a matter of life and death...I can assure them that it is much more serious than that.* (Dedicated to my Scottish brother and friend Alan Buntain)
* *Sure, luck means a lot in football. Not having a good striker is bad luck.*
* *My drinking team has a soccer problem.*

Forgiveness

* *The stupid neither forgive nor forget; the naïve forgive and forget; the wise forgive but do not forget.*
* *Forgive your enemies...if you can't get back at them any other way.*
* *If I die, I forgive you: if I recover, we shall see.*

Friendship

* *John has always been there...when he has needed me.*
* *God save me from my friends – I can protect myself from my enemies.*
* *Friendship improves happiness and abates misery by doubling our joy and dividing our grief.*

Gambling

* *My wife left me because I am addicted to gambling. There must be something I can do...to win her back.*

* *Life is a gamble at terrible odds. If it was a bet…you wouldn't take it.*
* *Nobody has ever bet enough on a winning horse.*

Genius

* *The difference between stupidity and genius is that genius has its limits.*
* *The public is wonderfully tolerant. It will forgive everything except genius.*
* *Genius is one per cent inspiration and ninety-nine per cent perspiration.*

Gentiles

* *The Jews were a proud people and throughout history they had trouble with unsympathetic genitals.* (Schoolboy)
* *'I am worried about my son. He is constantly playing with his genitals.'*
  'Don't worry about it, Darling. Some of my best friends are genitals.'
* *Gentile is a polite term for anyone who doesn't love a good bargain or has extra skin on his twinkie.*

Gentlemen

* *A true gentleman never swears at his wife when ladies are present.*
* *A true gentleman knows how to play the bagpipes…but doesn't.*
* *With a gentleman I am always a gentleman and a half, and with a fraud I try to be a fraud and a half.*

God

* When we talk to God, that is praying, but should God speak to us…that would be paranoid schizophrenia.
* *Everyman believes God to be on his side…but only the rich and powerful know that he really is.*
* *'What makes you think that you are God?'*
  'Simple. Every time I speak to him I find I am talking to myself.'

Goodness

* *Treat those who are good with goodness, and also treat those who are not good with goodness. Thus goodness is attained. Be honest to those who are honest, and be also honest to those who are not honest. Thus honesty is attained …*
* *It is better to be beautiful than to be good. But it is definitely better to be good than to be ugly.*
* *If you pretend to be good, the world takes you very seriously. If you pretend to be bad, it doesn't. Such is the astounding stupidity of optimism.*

Gossip

* *Gossip is the art of saying nothing in a way that leaves practically nothing unsaid.*
* *Gossip is when you hear something you like about someone you don't.*
* *Some people approach every problem with an open mouth.*

Government

* *All the people who know how to run the country are busy driving cabs or cutting hair.*
* *The Government's solution to a problem is often as bad as the problem itself.*
* *You can fool too many of the people too much of the time.*

Grandparents

* *Maybe there is no actual place called hell. Maybe hell is just having to listen to our grandparents breathe through their noses when they're eating sandwiches*
* *The reason grandparents and grandchildren get along so well is that they have a common enemy.*
* *The simplest toy, one which even the youngest child can operate, is called a grandparent.*

Guests

*   It's better to leave while staying is welcomed than to stay while leaving is welcomed.
*   Isn't it amazing how nice people are to you when they know you're leaving?
*   Everyone has the ability of making someone happy; some by entering the room, others by leaving it.

Happiness

*   Happiness is no laughing matter.
*   My life has no purpose, no direction, no aim, no meaning and yet I am happy. I cannot figure it out. What am I doing right?
*   Men who are unhappy, like men who sleep badly, are always proud of the fact.

Hate

*   Hate is such a luxurious emotion it can only be spent on one we love.
*   You know that when I hate you, it is because I love you to a point of passion that unhinges my soul.
*   I love you, and because I love you, I would sooner have you hate me for telling you the truth than adore me for telling you lies.

Health

*   The one sure way to remain healthy is to drink what you do not like, eat what you do not want and do all the things that you would rather not.
*   Why is it that everything good is illegal, immoral or fattening?
*   Had I known I would live this long I would have taken better care of myself.

History

*   History is a hard core of interpretation surrounded by a pulp of disputable facts.

* *Well-behaved women rarely make history.*
* *History doesn't repeat itself – at best it sometimes rhymes.*

Honesty

* *Beware of him; he is likely to go behind you in revolving doors and come out ahead.*
* *It is a fine thing to be honest, but it is also very important to be right.*
* *Integrity is telling myself the truth. Honesty is telling the truth to other people.*

Housework

* *A man's idea of housework is to sweep the room with a glance.*
* *There is but an hour a day between a good housewife and a bad one.*
* *There is no need to do any housework at all. After four years the dirt doesn't get any worse.*

Humour

* *Humour is a funny thing.*
* *I don't find humour funny.*
* *Grant me a sense of humour, Lord*
  The saving grace to see a joke,
  To win some happiness from life
  And pass it on to other folk.

Hunger

* *A good meal ought to begin with hunger.*
* *Success without honour is an unseasoned dish; it will satisfy your hunger, but it won't taste good.*
* *The hunger for love is much more difficult to remove than the hunger for bread.*

Husband

* *A husband is what is left of a lover after the nerve has been extracted.*

* *Husbands are like fire…they tend to go out if unattended.*
* *Husbands are a small band of men, armed only with wallets, besieged by a horde of wives and children.*

Hypochondria
* *The trouble with being a hypochondriac these days is that antibiotics have cured all the good diseases.*
* *The best cure for hypochondria is to forget about your body and get interested in someone else's.*
* *Hypochondria is the only disease I haven't got.*

Ignorance
* *It isn't that John is ignorant; it is that he knows so much that isn't so.*
* *Consistency requires you to be as ignorant today as you were a year ago.*
* *What he doesn't know would make a library anybody would be proud of.*

Illness
* *I have got Parkinson's disease…and he has got mine.*
* *There are some remedies worse than the disease.*
* *One of the minor pleasures of life is to be slightly ill.*

Imagination
* *John often mistakes his imagination for his memory.*
* *The man who has no imagination has no wings.*
* *The true sign of intelligence is not knowledge but imagination.*

Impression
* *You never get a second chance to make a good impression.*
* *Don't be over self-confident with your first impressions of people.*
* *Sometimes one creates a dynamic impression by saying something, and sometimes one creates as significant an impression by remaining silent.*

Insanity

* I don't suffer from insanity…I enjoy every minute of it.
* Earth is the insane asylum for the universe.
* Insane people are always sure they're just fine. It is only the sane people who are willing to admit they are crazy.

Insurance

* Insurance is what you pay for all your life so that you can die rich.
* Fun is like life insurance…the older you get, the more it costs.
* Unemployment insurance is a pre-paid vacation for freeloaders.

Intellectuals

* An intellectual is someone who has found something more interesting than sex.
* People who refer to themselves as intellectuals are committing a social crime as well as an error.
* To be honest what I feel bad about is that I do not feel worse. That is the intellectual's problem in a nutshell.

Intelligence

* John is really clever, but sometimes he allows his brains to go to his head.
* John has a brilliant mind…until he makes it up.
* Dolphins are so highly intelligent that they are known, within a few days of their captivity, to train humans to stand on the edge of their pool and throw them fish three times a day.

Internet

* It was always said that a million monkeys banging on a million typewriters would eventually produce the complete works of Shakespeare. Now, thanks to the internet, we know that this is not true.
* The trouble with the internet is that it's replacing masturbation as a leisure activity.

* *The internet is useless. It can only give you answers.*

Invention
* *Percy Shaw invented the 'cat's eye' in 1933 when he saw a cat, with bright eyes shining, walking towards him. Had the cat been walking away from him, he may well have invented the pencil sharpener.*
* *We owe a lot to Thomas Edison – if it wasn't for him we would be watching television by candlelight.*
* *Invention is the talent of youth, as judgement is of age.*

Jazz
* *If you have to ask what jazz is, you will never know.*
* *Jazz tickles your muscles; symphonies stretch your soul.*
* *Jazz is the only music in which the same note can be played night after night but differently each time.*

Jealousy
* *Jealousy springs more from love of self than from love of another.*
* *Jealousy is all the fun you think they had.*
* *Jealousy, that dragon which slays love under the pretence of keeping it alive.*

Jesus
* *Jesus was born because Mary had an immaculate contraption.* (Schoolboy)
* *No one ever made more trouble than the 'gentle Jesus meek and mild'.*
* *Jesus died too soon. If he had lived to my age he would have repudiated his doctrine.*

Jewel
* *If I could be granted a wish, I'd shine in your eye like a jewel.*
* *The earth is like a beautiful bride who needs no man-made jewels to heighten her loveliness.*
* *Plain dealing is a jewel, but they that wear it are out of fashion.*

Jews
* *If you ever forget you are a Jew, a gentile will remind you.*
* *How odd of God*
  To choose the Jews;
  Not half as odd, by God,
  For Gentiles a Jewish God to choose
  (Maybe not so odd of God...Goyim annoy Him.)
* *To calculate the date according to the Jewish calendar you need to take the current Anno Domini and add interest.*

Journalism
* *Journalism is the first rough draft of history.*
* *Journalists make it a point to know very little about an extremely wide variety of topics; that is how they stay objective.*
* *Journalism allows its readers to witness history; fiction gives its readers an opportunity to live it.*

Judging
* *The more you judge, the less you love.*
* *When we judge or criticise another person, it says nothing about that person; it merely says something about our own need to be critical.*
* *We are all inclined to judge ourselves by our ideals, others by their acts.*

Jury
* *A jury consists of twelve persons chosen to decide who has the better lawyer.*
* *A jury is a group of twelve people of average ignorance.*
* *The hungry judges soon the sentence sign*
  and wretches hang that jurymen may dine.

Justice
* *Everybody wants to see justice done...to somebody else.*

* *Justice always prevails…three times out of seven.*
* *We want an indictment. We want justice.*

Juveniles
* *Juvenile delinquency would disappear if kids followed their parent's advice instead of their example*
* *Our hamburgers, made from the flesh of chemically impregnated cattle, had been broiled over counterfeit charcoal, placed between slices of artificially flavoured cardboard and served to us by recycled juvenile delinquents.*
* *Juvenile delinquency is a modern term for what we did when we were kids.*

Key
* *Love is the master key which opens the gates of happiness.*
* *The key is to get to know people and trust them to be who they are. Instead, we trust people to be who we want them to be – and when they're not, we cry.*
* *The key to immortality is first living a life worth remembering.*

Kicking
* *Men kick friendship around like a football but it doesn't seem to break. Women treat it like glass and it goes to pieces.*
* *A cat is a soft, indestructible automaton provided by nature to be kicked when things go wrong in the domestic circle.*
* *You may not realise it when it happens, but a kick in the teeth may be the best thing in the world for you.*

Kidneys
* *The kidneys are the exciters of sexual desire for the veins which empty into the testicles pass directly through the kidneys, deriving hence a certain pungency provocative of lust.*
* *This too shall pass – just like a kidney stone.*
* *A man of forty today has nothing to worry him but falling hair, inability to button the top button, failing vision, shortness of*

breath, a tendency of the collar to shut off all breathing, trembling of the kidneys to whatever tune the orchestra is playing, and a general sense of giddiness when the matter of rent is brought up. Forty is Life's Golden Age.

Kids

* *We worry about what a child will become tomorrow, yet we forget that he is someone today.*
* *You can learn many things from children. How much patience you have, for instance.*
* *A characteristic of the normal child is he doesn't act that way very often.*

Kindness

* *The smallest act of kindness is worth more than the grandest intention.*
* *Warm smile is the universal language of kindness.*
* *Kindness causes us to learn and to forget many things.*

Kings

* *All humane things are subject to decay and when fate summons kings must obey.*
* *When Kings through their bloodthirsty commanders lay waste a country, they dignify their atrocity by calling it 'making peace'.*
* *It is hard enough luck being a king, without being a target also.*

Kissing

* *Any man who can drive safely while kissing a pretty girl is simply not giving the kiss the attention it deserves.*
* *Happiness is like a kiss...you must share it to enjoy it.*
* *A kiss is a lovely trick designed by nature to stop speech when words become superfluous.*

Kitchen

* *If you can't stand the heat, get out of the kitchen.*

* *I have a greater appreciation for kitchen appliances, having played one.*
* *The trouble with my wife is that she is a whore in the kitchen and a cook in bed.*

Knees
* *I have been driven many times to my knees by the overwhelming conviction that I had nowhere to go. My own wisdom, and that of all about me, seemed insufficient for the day.*
* *Failures are like skinned knees: painful, but superficial.*
* *There are thoughts which are prayers. There are moments when, whatever the posture of the body, the soul is on its knees.*

Knowledge
* *What you don't know would make a great book.*
* *Those who think they know everything are very annoying to those of us who do.*
* *Even more exasperating than the guy who thinks he knows it all is the one who really does.*

Language
* *Speech happens not to be his language.*
* *He speaks ten languages…all of them in English.*
* *He speaks at least eight languages and he says nothing in all of them.*

Laughter
* *He who laughs lasts …*
* *Laughter is the shortest distance between two people.*
* *He who laughs last…probably didn't get the joke.*

Law
* *The Law is the true embodiment*
  Of everything that is excellent.
  It has no kind of fault or flaw,
  And I, my Lords, embody the Law.

* *I have only been ruined twice in my life – first time when I lost a court case and second time, when I won one.*
* *I inherited what my father called the Art of the Advocate: or the irritating habit of looking for the flaw in any argument*

Laziness
* *A wishbone will never take the place of a backbone.*
* *One of these days is none of these days.*
* *The hardest work is to go idle.*

Lecture
* *The secret of a good lecture is to appear to have known all your life what you learnt this afternoon.*
* *Speaking comes more easily if you have something to say.*
* *A good portion of speaking will consist in knowing how to lie.*

Lies
* *A misleading impression is not a lie…it is being economical with the truth.*
* *If he stops telling lies about me…I will stop telling the truth about him.*
* *A half-truth is a whole lie.*

Life
* *Many people are alive only because it's illegal to shoot them.*
* *It is better to have lived and loved, than never to have lived at all.*
* *The mystery of life lies in the universe and the universe is like a safe to which there is a combination. The combination, however, is locked up in the safe.*

Logic
* *In any given set of circumstances, the proper course of action is determined by subsequent events.*
* *Logic is the art of thinking and reasoning in strict accordance with the limitations and incapacities of human misunderstanding.*

*   *Logic is a systematic method of coming to the wrong conclusion with confidence.*

Love
*   *A man is only as good as what he loves.*
*   *Love is like the measles – all the worse when it comes late in life.*
*   *When a woman has given you her heart – it is impossible to get rid of the rest of her body.*

Luck
*   *The luck for having talent is not enough; one must also have talent for having luck.*
*   *The odds are five to six that the light at the end of the tunnel is the headlight of an oncoming train.*
*   *May bad luck follow you all your days...and never catch up with you.*

Marriage
*   *John is happily married...but his wife isn't.*
*   *By all means, marry. If you get a good wife, you'll become happy; if you get a bad one, you'll become a philosopher.*
*   *Christians have only one spouse. This is called monotony.* (Schoolboy)

Masons
*   *Old Masons never die,*
    and you have to join to find out why.
*   *To raise the weak, restrain the strong,*
    To chase the tear from sorrow's eye;
    To aid the right, to check the wrong;
    And bid the weary cease to sigh;
    To soothe the orphan's mournful cry,
    A brother's help where're he be;
    To love all men beneath the sky,
    This is the bond of Masonry.
*   *A Freemason is not a man who builds houses free of charge.*

Melancholy

* *A patient goes to the doctor complaining of melancholy. After consultation the doctor says: 'You need amusement. Why don't you go and see the comedian Grimaldi. He will make you laugh and that is the best medicine.' The patient replies: 'I am Grimaldi!'*
* *There is no such thing as happiness, only lesser shades of melancholy.*
* *It is a melancholy truth that even great men have their poor relations.*

Memory

* *Let us forget it never happened.*
* *To look is to forget the names of the things you have seen.*
* *I remember your name perfectly...but I just can't think of your face.*

Middle Age

* *Middle age is when faced with two temptations you select the one that will get you home earlier.*
* *When I was young I had success with women because I was young. Now I am old, I have success with women because I am old. Middle age was the hardest part.*
* *You've reached middle age when all you exercise is caution.*

Modesty

* *Modesty is a good quality, but it can be overdone.*
* *Do not be so modest...you are not as important as you think.*
* *I often wished I had time to cultivate modesty...but I am too busy thinking about myself.*

Money

* *Why is it that there is so much month left at the end of the money?*

* *Money isn't everything…but it is a long way ahead of what comes next.*
* *Money cannot buy happiness but it's more comfortable to cry in a Mercedes than on a bicycle.*

Mothers

* *God could not be everywhere and therefore he made mothers.*
* *An ounce of mother is worth a pound of clergy.*
* *Of the two lots, the woman's lot of perpetual motherhood, and the man's of perpetual babyhood, I prefer the man's.*

Mother-in-Law

* *Behind every successful man…is a surprised mother-in-law.*
* *Adam was the luckiest man; he had no mother-in-law.*
* *I should, many a good day, have blown my brains out, but for the recollection that it would have given pleasure to my mother-in-law; and, even then, if I could have been certain to haunt her – but I won't dwell upon these trifling family matters.*

Music

* *John may not like music, but he loves the noise it makes.*
* *'Can I speak to the Bank Manager, please?' 'I am afraid the Bank Manager died over the weekend. He has not been replaced.'*
  'Can I speak to the Bank Manager?'
  'Sir, I just said the Bank Manager is dead…why do you keep asking?'
  'Because it is like music to my ears!'
* *There is too much sax and violins in music.*

Names

* *Why name him Jerome?…Every Tom, Dick and Harry is named Jerome.*
* *Nicknames stick to people, and the most ridiculous are the most adhesive.*
* *What's in a name? That which we call a rose by any other name would smell as sweet.*

Narcissism

* He fell in love with himself at first sight and it is a passion to which he has always remained faithful.
* A narcissist is someone who is better looking than you are.
* Even though friends say they are interested in your life, they never really want to talk about you as much as you want them to.

Navy

* The Royal Navy of England hath ever been its greatest defence and ornament; it is its ancient and natural strength; the floating bulwark of the island.
* I enlisted when I was a boy. The Navy looked after me like my mother. It fed me, took care of me and gave me wonderful opportunities.
* The only colour I don't have is navy brown.

Negotiation

* If women ran the world we wouldn't have wars, just intense negotiations every 28 days.
* Flattery is the infantry of negotiation.
* Negotiations are a euphemism for capitulation if the shadow of power is not cast across the bargaining table.

Neurosis

* A neurosis is a secret you do not know you are keeping.
* I love her too, but our neuroses just don't match.
* I have taken 40 years to make my psychology simple. I might say all neurosis is vanity – but this also might not be understood.

Neutrality

* The hottest places in hell are reserved for those who in a period of moral crisis maintain their neutrality.
* Neutrality is at times a graver sin than belligerence.
* Even to observe neutrality you must have a strong government.

Newspapers

* *I keep reading between the lies.*
* *I read the newspaper avidly. It is my one form of continuous fiction.*
* *People everywhere confuse what you read in the newspaper with news.*

No-no

* *'Every time I sneeze I have an orgasm.'*
  'What do you do about it?'
  'I take snuff.'
* *God gave men both a penis and a brain, but unfortunately not enough blood supply to run both at the same time.*
* *Masturbation is the primary sexual activity of mankind: in the 19th century it was a disease, now it is a cure.*

Noise

* *Don't get annoyed when your neighbour plays his hi-fi at two in the morning…call him at five and tell him how much you enjoyed it.*
* *Noise has been defined as a stench in the ear – the chief product and authentication of civilisation.*
* *Please explain why your silence makes more noise than thunder.*

Nudity

* *Don't miss our show: six beautiful girls, five beautiful swimsuits.*
* *The problem with dancing in the nude is that not everything stops when the music does.*
* *Full frontal nudity is now the norm in every branch of the theatre and entertainment…with the possible exception of lady accordion players.*

Obscenity

* Indecency, vulgarity, obscenity – these are strictly confined to man; he invented them. Among the higher animals there is no trace of them.
* Of all the strange 'crimes' that human beings have legislated of nothing, 'blasphemy' is the most amazing – with 'obscenity' and 'indecent exposure' fighting it out for the second and third place.
* Obscenity is the sign of a weak mind trying to express itself.

Obstinacy

* The difference between perseverance and obstinacy is that one often comes from a strong will, and the other from a strong won't.
* That which is called firmness in a king is called obstinacy in a donkey.
* Love is the only fire that is hot enough to melt the iron obstinacy of a creature's will.

Occult

* I like to browse in occult bookshops if for no other reason than to refresh my commitment to science.
* Divination is the art of nosing out the occult. Divination is of as many kinds as there are fruit-bearing varieties of the flowering dunce and the early fool.
* The ancient philosophies were of two kinds: 'exoteric', those that the philosophers themselves could partly understand, and 'esoteric', those that nobody could understand. It is the latter that have most profoundly affected modern thought and found greatest acceptance in our time. Esotericism is a very particularly abstruse and consummate aspect of the occult.

Office

* An office is where you go to relax after a strenuous home life.
* What you're seeing in the office market is that there is more demand for office space than there is space. The market is very, very strong.

* *They've finally come up with the perfect office computer. If it makes a mistake, it blames another computer.*

Old Age
* *One problem with getting older is that it gets progressively more difficult to find a famous historical figure who did not amount to much when he was your age.*
* *The older I get…the better I used to be.*
* *We do not stop playing because we get old…we get old because we stop playing.*

Opera
* *Opera is when a guy gets stabbed and instead of bleeding…he sings.*
* *If you were to suppress adultery, fanaticism, crime, evil, the supernatural from opera, there would no longer be the means for writing one note.*
* *Going to the opera, like getting drunk, is a sin that carries its own punishment with it.*

Opinion
* *My opinions may have changed, but not the fact that I am right.*
* *No woman ever falls in love with a man unless she has a better opinion of him than he deserves.*
* *Do not fear to be eccentric in opinion, for every opinion now accepted was once eccentric.*

Opportunity
* *Jumping at several small opportunities may get us there more quickly than waiting for one big one to come along.*
* *Opportunity is often difficult to recognise; we usually expect it to beckon us with beepers and billboards.*
* *Opportunities fly by while we sit regretting the chances we have lost, and the happiness that comes to us we heed not, because of the happiness that is gone.*

Optimism

* *I knew of a man who planned to sell his house and carried a brick in his pocket to show as a pattern to potential buyers.*
* *I am an optimist. It does not seem too much use being anything else.*
* *Both optimists and pessimists contribute to our society. The optimist invents the aeroplane and the pessimist the parachute.*

Overweight

* *Imprisoned in every fat man, a thin one is wildly signalling to be let out.*
* *Obesity is really wide spread.*
* *The body of a young woman is God's greatest achievement…he could have built it to last a little longer, though…but you can't have everything.*

Paranoia

* *Just because you're not paranoid doesn't mean they're not out to get you.*
* *Perfect paranoia is perfect awareness.*
* *A paranoiac, like a poet, is born, not made.*

Pessimist

* *A pessimist is one who when he has the choice of two evils, chooses both.*
* *A pessimist sees the difficulty in every opportunity; an optimist sees the opportunity in every difficulty.*
* *A pessimist is a man who has been compelled to live with an optimist.*

Philosophy

* *Question: I have come to ask a question: what is the best question that can be asked and the best answer given?*
  Answer: The best question that can be asked is the one you ask and the best answer is the one I am giving.

* *Experience has shown, and a true philosophy will always show, that a vast, perhaps the larger, portion of the truth arises from the seemingly irrelevant.*
* *What is the first business of philosophy? To part with self-conceit. For it is impossible for anyone to begin to learn what he thinks that he already knows.*

Pleasure
* *Life would be very pleasant if it were not for its enjoyments.*
* *There is no cure for birth or death…except to enjoy the interval between the two.*
* *Yesterday is history and tomorrow a mystery…so enjoy today.*

Politics
* *Politics is supposed to be the second oldest profession. I have come to realise that it bears a very close resemblance to the first.*
* *Politics is the art of preventing people from taking part in affairs which properly concerns them.*
* *A good politician is one who understands and runs government. A statesman is a politician who has been dead 10 to 15 years.*

Poverty
* *I am fond of poverty. If it weren't so costly, I would treat myself to it.*
* *In a country well governed, poverty is something to be ashamed of. In a country badly governed, wealth is something to be ashamed of.*
* *Anyone who has ever struggled with poverty knows how extremely expensive it is to be poor.*

Prayer
* *Lord, lord, lord. Protect me from the consequences of the above prayer.*
* *May those who love us love us,*
  And those who do not love us,

> *May God turn their hearts*
> *And if He cannot turn their hearts*
> *May He turn their ankles*
> *That we may know them by their limping.*

* *Prayer carries us halfway to God, fasting brings us to the door of his palace and alms-giving procures us admission.*

Promises

* *A verbal contract isn't worth the paper it's written on.*
* *The man who promises everything is sure to fulfil nothing, and everyone who promises too much is in danger of using evil means in order to carry out his promises, and is already on the road to perdition.*
* *We promise according to our hopes, and perform according to our fears.*

Psychology

* *Psychology is the study of those that do not need studying by those that do.*
* *Our heads are round so that thought can change direction.*
* *All despotisms should be considered problems of mental hygiene, and all support of censorship should be considered as problems of abnormal psychology.*

Public Relations

* *Some are born great, some achieve greatness and some hire a public relations officer.*
* *Public opinion, though often formed upon a wrong basis, yet generally has a strong underlying sense of justice.*
* *Health is the greatest gift, contentment the greatest wealth, faithfulness the best relationship.*

Quality

* *I am easily satisfied with the very best.*
* *Charm is the quality in others that makes us more satisfied with ourselves.*

*   *Quality is not an act, it is a habit.*

Quarrel
*   *A quarrel between friends, when made up, adds a new tie to friendship.*
*   *War is a quarrel between two thieves too cowardly to fight their own battle.*
*   *The test of a man or woman's breeding is how they behave in a quarrel.*

Queen
*   *England or Great Britain as it is known more popularly, is a land which has for long been a home to people belonging to a number of different cultures and races. The tolerance that it has for different people is in itself immense. Today it also holds the position of the financial capital of the world and is also a part of the European Union. It has for long been a colonial power which has ruled over many nations. It is home to the famous Queen Elizabeth and her descendants. With splendid countryside and cold weather, it is a very much sought after destination by the youth of the Asian countries. In spite of their hats being very ugly, Goddam! I love the English.*
*   *I was a queen, and you took away my crown; a wife, and you killed my husband; a mother, and you deprived me of my children. My blood alone remains: take it, but do not make me suffer long.*
*   *A beautiful woman can be painted as a totem only; not as a woman, but as a Madonna, a queen, a sphinx.*

Queer
*   *There are certain queer times and occasions in this strange mixed affair we call life when a man takes his whole universe for a vast practical joke.*
*   *The only queer people are those who don't love anybody.*

* *Girls are so queer you never know what they mean. They say 'No' when they mean 'Yes' and drive a man out of his wits for the fun of it.*

Questions
* *The one real object of education is to have a man in the condition of continually asking questions.*
* *Love is the answer, but while you are waiting for the answer sex raises some pretty good questions.*
* *You can tell whether a man is clever by his answers. You can tell whether a man is wise by his questions.*

Questions (2)
* *Sometimes the questions are complicated and the answers are simple.*
* *He who asks a question is a fool for five minutes; he who does not ask a question remains a fool forever.*
* *The wise man questions the wisdom of others because he questions his own; the foolish man, because it is different from his own.*

Quiet
* *I thoroughly disapprove of duels. If a man should challenge me, I would take him kindly and forgivingly by the hand and lead him to a quiet place and kill him.*
* *Men would live exceedingly quiet if these two words, 'mine and thine' were taken away.*
* *Religion is excellent stuff for keeping common people quiet.*

Quotations
* *A book of quotations…can never be complete.*
* *Most anthologists of quotations are like those who eat cherries or oysters: first picking the best ones and winding up by eating everything.* (Dedicated to myself, the author of this booklet)
* *Quotations will tell the full measure of meaning, if you have enough of them.*

Race
* *Racial superiority is a mere pigment of the imagination.*
* *One day our descendants will think it incredible that we paid so much attention to things like the amount of melanin in our skin or the shape of our eyes or our gender instead of the unique identities of each of us as complex human beings.*
* *The conquest of the earth, which mostly means the taking it away from those who have a different complexion or slightly flatter noses than ourselves, is not a pretty thing when you look into it.*

Railways
* *Sunday morning, although recurring at regular and well foreseen intervals, always seems to take this railway by surprise.*
* *People's backyards are much more interesting than their front gardens, and houses that back on to railways are public benefactors.*
* *When you are on a railway station platform waiting for the train that is due, and when you discover that it is five hours late, how do you react? You swear at the train.*

Reading
* *If you can read this, thank a teacher.*
* *Reading is sometimes an ingenious device for avoiding thought.*
* *To read is to fly: it is to soar to a point of vantage which gives a view over wide terrains of history, human variety, ideas, shared experience and the fruits of many inquiries.*

Recommendation
* *Good men need no recommendation and bad men…it wouldn't help.*
* *Personal beauty is a greater recommendation than any letter of introduction.*
* *A good face, they say, is a letter of recommendation. O Nature,*

Nature, why art thou so dishonest, as ever to send men with these false recommendations into the World.

Regret

* *The follies a man most regrets in his life are those he did not commit when the opportunity arose.*
* *Live your life without regret, don't be someone who they'll forget.*
* *When loving someone, never regret what you do, only regret what you don't do.*

Relatives

* *When our relatives are at home, we have to think of all their good points or it would be impossible to endure them. But when they are away, we console ourselves for their absence by dwelling on their vices.*
* *It isn't necessary to have relatives in town in order to be unhappy.*
* *All people are your relatives, therefore expect only trouble from them.*

Religion

* *My husband and I divorced over religious differences. He thought he was God and I didn't.*
* *What a pity that we have no amusements in England, except for vice and religion.*
* *Religion is an insult to human dignity. With or without it, you'd have good people doing good things and evil people doing bad things, but for good people to do bad things, it takes religion.*

Research

* *Researchers have discovered that chocolate produces some of the same reactions in the brain as marijuana. The researchers also discovered other similarities between the two but can't remember what they are.*
* *Use one source and it is plagiarism; use two and it is research.*

* *Science too often trivialises the profound, answering questions that are very different from the ones that were asked. To formulate a question suitable for scientific research too often requires us to forget what it was that we really wanted to know.*

Responsibility
* *Perhaps it is better to be irresponsible and right, than to be responsible and wrong.*
* *If you want children to keep their feet on the ground, put some responsibility on their shoulders.*
* *Responsibility: A detachable burden easily shifted to the shoulders of God, Fate, Fortune, Luck or one's neighbour. In the days of astrology it was customary to unload it upon a star.*

Romance
* *Romance without finance…is no good.*
* *Romance has been elegantly defined as the offspring of fiction and love.*
* *When one is in love, one always begins by deceiving one's self, and one always ends by deceiving others. That is what the world calls a romance.*

Sarcasm
* *Sarcasm is the greatest weapon of the smallest mind.*
* *Sarcasm is the lowest form of wit.*
* *There are many kinds of smiles, each having a distinct character. Some announce goodness and sweetness, others betray sarcasm, bitterness and pride; some soften the countenance by their languishing tenderness, others brighten by their spiritual vivacity.*

Secrets
* *A secret is what we tell everybody not to tell anybody.*
* *He that has eyes to see and ears to hear may convince himself that no mortal can keep a secret. If his lips are silent, he chatters with his fingertips; betrayal oozes out of him at every pore.*

* *Whoever wishes to keep a secret must hide the fact that he possesses one.*

Silence
* *I believe in the discipline of silence…and I could talk for hours about it.*
* *He has occasional flashes of silence that make his conversation absolutely delightful*
* *A good time to keep your mouth shut is when you're in deep water.*

Sleep
* *John hasn't slept for months. That is why he goes to bed early. One needs more rest when one does not sleep.*
* *Sometimes I lie awake at night, and I ask: 'Where have I gone wrong?' Then a voice says to me, 'This is going to take more than one night.'*
* *Sleep faster, we need the pillows.*

Smoking
* *Thank you for not smoking. Cigarette smoke is the residue of your pleasure. It contaminates the air, pollutes my hair and clothes, not to mention my lungs. This takes place without my consent. I have a pleasure, also. I like a beer now and then. The residue of my pleasure is urine. Would you be annoyed if I stood on a chair and pissed on your head and your clothes without your consent?*
* *Smoking is a dying habit.*
* *A good cigar is as much comfort to a man as a good cry is to a woman.* (Dedicated to my close and excellent friend Edward Sahakian)

Speaking
* *Say what you have to say and the first time you come to a sentence with a break…stop talking.*
* *The secret of a good speech is to have a good beginning and a*

good ending; and to have the two as close together as possible.
* *Eating words has never given me indigestion.*

Statistics

* *A recent survey has proved that smoking is the greatest cause of statistics.*
* *In ancient times they had no statistics so they had to fall back on lies.*
* *I always find that statistics are hard to swallow and impossible to digest. The only one I can ever remember is that if all the people who go to sleep in church were laid end-to-end they would be a lot more comfortable.*

Success

* *I have no idea what the formula for success is. The formula for failure, however, is 'try to please everybody'.*
* *All you need is ignorance and confidence, and success is assured.*
* *Coming together is a beginning; keeping together is progress; working together is success.*

Suicide

* *I was so depressed last night thinking about the economy, wars, jobs, my savings, Social Security, retirement funds, and our bleak future, that I called the Suicide Lifeline and was connected to a call centre in Pakistan. When I told them I was suicidal, they got all excited, and asked if I could drive a truck.*
* *Suicide is man's way of telling God, 'You can't fire me – I quit.'*
* *Suicide is the sincerest form of criticism life gets.*

Superstition

* *Trust the rabbit's foot if you will, but remember it didn't work for the rabbit.*
* *'I didn't think you were superstitious.' – 'I am not…but this rabbit's foot <u>really</u> works!'*
* *The root of all superstition is that men observe when a thing hits, but not when it misses.*

Teeth

*   *If you can't bite, don't show your teeth.*
*   *Love and toothache have many cures, but none infallible, except possession and dispossession.*
*   *You don't have to brush your teeth – just the ones you want to keep.*

Telephone

*   *In a gym the mobile phone rings and John answers: 'Yes, darling…£2,000? That is OK, buy and enjoy…another £5K? Don't worry; you can use my credit card. See you later, sweetie.' He shuts the mobile phone, holds it high and says: 'Whose phone is this?'*
*   *'If the phone rings, under no circumstances say that I am at home' says a concerned husband to his wife. The phone rings. 'My husband is at home.' replies the wife and puts the phone down. Before the irate husband has a chance to utter a word, she says: 'Don't worry, that was for me not for you.'*
*   *Mobile phones are the only subject on which men boast about who's got the smallest.*

Television

*   *If it weren't for electricity we'd all be watching television by candlelight.*
*   *So many TV interviews appear to consist of people who cannot write interviewing people who cannot talk for an audience who cannot read.*
*   *Television is chewing gum for the eyes.*

Temptation

*   *Lead me not into temptation; I can find the way myself.*
*   *I can resist anything…except for temptation.*
*   *Abstainer: a weak person who yields to the temptation of denying himself a pleasure.*

Time
* *Time is what keeps everything from happening all at once.*
* *You certainly cannot turn back the clock…but you can wind it up again.*
* *Time is man's most precious asset.*

Tolerance
* *Tolerance is a great trait to contain, but so is the ability to shut up.*
* *In people, just as in machines, tolerance permits a maximum of efficiency with a minimum of friction.*
* *Excessive tolerance is complicity.*

Tomorrow
* *Tomorrow is often the busiest day of the year.*
* *Never do today what you can put off till tomorrow.*
* *We are tomorrow's past.*

Travel
* *Every year it takes less time to fly across the world and more time to drive to the office.*
* *Travel is 90% anticipation and 10% recollection.*
* *A journey of a thousand miles must begin with a single step.*

Truth
* *Some people relate to truth carelessly…others never touch it at all.*
* *Comments are free, but facts…they are on expenses.*
* *A truth ceases to be true when more than one person believes in it.*

Understanding
* *I know that you believe you understand what you think I said, but I'm not sure you realise that what you heard is not what I meant.*
* *I am so clever that sometimes I don't understand a single word of what I am saying.*

* *All truths are easy to understand once they are discovered; the point is to discover them.*

Union
* *The three ingredients of a successful union between two… humour, commitment and undying love.*
* *At the innermost core of all loneliness is a deep and powerful yearning for union with one's lost self.*
* *The most happy marriage I can imagine would be the union of a deaf man to a blind woman.*

Universal
* *Humour is a universal language.*
* *I would rather believe all the fables and the legends in the Talmud and the Koran and the Bible, than that this universal frame is without a mind.*
* *There are three universal languages: love, music and sport.*

Unknown
* *People are supposed to fear the unknown, but ignorance is bliss when knowledge is so damn frightening.*
* *They are ill discoverers that think there is no land, because they can see nothing but sea.*
* *One is never afraid of the unknown; one is afraid of the known coming to an end.*

Utopia
* *Hell is like Utopia…but with central heating.*
* *Abandon all hopes of Utopia – there are people involved.*
* *Perhaps the greatest Utopia would be if we could all realise that no Utopia is possible; no place to run, no place to hide, just take care of business here and now.*

Value

* A man will pay £2 for a £1 item that he wants. A woman will pay £2 for a £1 item that she doesn't want.
* Until you value yourself, you won't value your time. Until you value your time, you will not do anything with it.
* We do not know the true value of our moments until they have undergone the test of memory.

Vanity

* Nothing makes one so vain as being told one is a sinner. Conscience makes egotists of us all.
* We are so vain that we even care for the opinion of those we don't care for.
* Vanity is my favourite sin.

Vegetables

* Please understand the reason why Chinese vegetables taste so good. It is simple. The Chinese do not cook them, they just threaten them.
* People need trouble – a little frustration to sharpen the spirit on, toughen it. Artists do; I don't mean you need to live in a rat hole or gutter, but you have to learn fortitude, endurance. Only vegetables are happy.
* Vegetables are interesting but lack a sense of purpose when unaccompanied by a good cut of meat.

Vegetarians

* I am not a vegetarian because I love animals. I am a vegetarian because I hate plants.
* Vegetarians eat vegetables – I am a humanitarian.
* A vegetarian is a person who won't eat anything that can have children.

Veterinarian

* *If having a soul means being able to feel love and loyalty and gratitude, then animals are better off than a lot of humans.*
* *Cats are connoisseurs of comfort.*
* *He was struck off the register for interfering with his patients. Great pity because he was a really good vet.*

Vice

* *When vice got the name of virtue, propriety was lost.*
* *There are vices of the time and vices of the individual.*
* *He has all the virtues I dislike and none of the vices I admire.*

Victory

* *Each victory is the summary of many defeats.*
* *Victory always starts in the head. It's a state of mind. It then spreads with such radiance and such affirmations that destiny can do nothing but obey.*
* *Triumph is just try with a little umph added.*

Virginity

* *It's kind of like virginity…it is hard to get back.*
* *I always thought of losing my virginity as a career move.*
* *Virginity for some women is the only virtue.*

Virtue

* *He has all the virtues I dislike and none of the vices I admire.*
* *Virtue is a beautiful thing in woman when they don't go about with it like a child with a drum making all sorts of noise with it.*
* *Virtue is praised, but hated. People run from it, for it is ice-cold and in this world you have to keep your feet warm.*

Vulgarity

* *Vulgarity is the conduct of other people, just as falsehoods are the truths of other people.*

* *Vulgarity has its uses. Vulgarity often cuts ice which refinement scrapes at vainly.*
* *Vulgarity is the rich man's modest contribution to democracy.*

Waiters
* *The best number for a dinner party is two; myself and a damn good head waiter.*
* *The British tourist is always happy abroad as long as the natives are waiters.*
* *I asked the waiter, 'Is this milk fresh?' He said, 'Sir, three hours ago it was grass.'*

War
* *War does not determine who is right – only who is left.*
* *The direct use of force is such a poor solution to any problem; it is generally employed only by small children and large nations.*
* *All the arms we need are for hugging.*

Wealth
* *'Tis better than riches*
  To scratch when it itches.'
* *Nobody in the world needs a mink coat…except a mink.*
* *To think we could be rich and not behave like the rich is like supposing that we could drink all day and remain absolutely sober.*

Weather
* *Sunshine is delicious, rain is refreshing, wind braces us up, snow is exhilarating; there is really no such thing as bad weather, only different kinds of good weather.*
* *The trouble with weather forecasting is that it's right too often for us to ignore it and wrong too often for us to rely on it.*
* *Weather is a great metaphor for life – sometimes it's good, sometimes it's bad, and there's nothing much you can do about it but carry an umbrella.*

Wedding

* *Wedlock or deadlock? That is the question.*
* *To keep your marriage brimming with love in the wedding cup, whenever you're wrong, admit it; whenever you're right, shut up.*
* *Our dog died from licking our wedding picture.*

Wisdom

* *Age is a high price to pay for maturity.*
* *Every man is a fool for at least five minutes every day; wisdom consists of not exceeding the limit.*
* *A smart person knows all the rules so he can break them wisely.*

Wives

* *Many men owe their success in life to their first wife…and their second wife to their success.*
* *My most brilliant achievement was my ability to be able to persuade my wife to marry me.*
* *A successful man is one who makes more money than his wife can spend. A successful woman is one who can find such a man.*

Woman

* *A woman is only a woman but a good cigar is a smoke.*
* *A woman without a man is like a fish without a bicycle.*
* *Love makes a fool of every man…and of every woman, a sage.*

Work

* *Choose a job you love, and you will never have to work a day in your life.*
* *Hard work pays off in the future. Laziness pays off now.*
* *Who says nothing is impossible. I've been doing nothing for years.*

Worry

* *Worries go down better with soup than without.*

* If you're in a bad situation, don't worry, it'll change. If you're in a good situation, don't worry, it'll change.
* Don't worry about life, you're not going to survive it anyway.

Xenophobia (an unreasonable fear of foreigners or strangers)
* Remember, remember always that all of us, and you and I especially, are descended from immigrants and revolutionists.
* I was raised to believe that excellence is the best deterrent to racism or sexism. And that's how I operate my life.
* Some of my best friends are foreigners.

Yachts
* Money can't buy you happiness, but it can buy you a yacht big enough to pull up right alongside it
* And next thing you're broke and the yacht that you got, it won't sail or float. You look back and try to catch someone's attention for help. You made a right at the light and they made a left…

Yawn
* A yawn may not be polite, but at least it is an honest opinion.
* A yawn is a silent shout.
* Please, keep talking. I always yawn when I am interested.

Year
* A lifetime should be counted in days and not in years.
* New Year is a harmless annual institution, of no particular use to anybody save as a scapegoat for promiscuous drunks, and friendly calls and humbug resolutions.
* The first of April is the day we remember what we are the other 364 days of the year.

Youth
* Youth is a disease from which we all recover. Also remembering that you are young only once but you can be immature all your life.

* *The youth of America is their oldest tradition…it has been going on now for 300 years…and I am not young enough to know everything.*
* *Our youth now loves luxury. They have bad manners, contempt for authority, disrespect for older people. Children nowadays are tyrants. They no longer rise when elders enter the room. They contradict their parents, chatter before company, gobble their food and tyrannise their teachers.*

  (Written <u>not</u> re the youth of today, as you would expect, but by Socrates in c400BC)

Zeal
* *Zeal is fit only for the wise but is found mostly in fools.*
* *Through zeal, knowledge is gotten; through lack of zeal, knowledge is lost.*
* *Zeal without knowledge is fire without light.*

Zebras
* *There's no end to the things you might know, depending how far beyond Zebra you go.*
* *If you hear hoof beats, look for horses, not zebras.*
* *The argument goes something like this:*
  'I refuse to prove that I exist,' says God, 'for proof denies faith, and without faith I am nothing.'
  'But,' says Man, 'the Babel fish is a dead giveaway, isn't it? It could not have evolved by chance. It proves you exist, and so therefore, by your own arguments, you don't.'
  'Oh dear,' says God, 'I hadn't thought of that' and promptly vanishes in a puff of logic.
  'Oh, that was easy,' says Man, and for an encore goes on to prove that black is white and gets himself killed on the next zebra crossing.

Zest

* *True happiness comes from the joy of deeds well done, the zest of creating things new.*

* *This bright New Year is given me*
  To live each day with zest …
  To daily grow and try to be
  My highest and my best!

* *What hunger is in relation to food, zest is in relation to life.*

Zip

* *Maybe men and women aren't from different planets as pop culture would have us believe. Maybe we live a lot closer to each other. Perhaps, dare I even say it, in the same zip code.*

* *Edward VIII replaced his fly buttons with a zip, a revolutionary move; and his Fair Isle pullovers, shorts and Windsor knots were considered by some to foreshadow the end of Empire.*

* *A dress that zips up the back will bring a husband and wife together.*

Zoo

* *Monkeys at the zoo should have to wear sunglasses so they can't hypnotise you.*

* *Jails and prisons are designed to break human beings, to convert the population into specimens in a zoo-obedient to our keepers, but dangerous to each other.*

* *A zoo is an excellent place to study the habits of human beings.*

Part 3

Freemasons' Immortal Words

COL. EDWIN BUZZ ALDRIN (1930-) Member of Montclair Lodge No. 144 in New Jersey. Awarded 32nd degree of the Ancient and Accepted Scottish Rite, Southern Jurisdiction, a Royal Arch Mason and Knight Templar in Authven Commandery, Houston, Texas. He received the Knight Templar Cross of Honour in 1969. American astronaut immortalised on 20 July 1969 when he followed Neil Armstrong down the ladder of Apollo 11 to be the second man on the moon…because he was farthest from the door of the lunar module 'Eagle'.

* *The eagle has landed!*
* *I think humans will reach Mars, and I would like to see it happen in my lifetime.*
* *We can continue to try and clean up the gutters all over the world and spend all of our resources looking at just the dirty spots and trying to make them clean. Or we can lift our eyes up and look into the skies and move forward in an evolutionary way.*

SALVADOR ALLENDE (1908-1973) Member of Lodge Progreso No. 4, Valparaiso, Chile in 1935. Chilean physician and politician. The first democratically elected Marxist to become President (1970-73) of a country in Latin America.

* *I have been to Cuba many times. I have spoken many times with Fidel Castro and got to know Ernesto Guevara fairly well. I know of Cuba's struggle and its leaders. But the situation in Cuba is very different from that in Chile. Cuba came from a dictatorship; I arrived at the presidency after being senator for 25 years.*

* *As for the bourgeois state, we are seeking to overcome it, to overthrow it.*
* *I am not the President of all the Chileans. I am not a hypocrite that says so.*

MUSTAFA KEMAL ATATÜRK (1881-1938) Initiated 1907 Macedonia Risorta Lodge No. 80 or Lodge Veritas, Thessaloniki, Greece under a *Grande Oriente d'Italia* warrant. Turkish army officer, revolutionary statesman and writer, founding father and first President of the Republic of Turkey.

* *A nation devoid of art and artists cannot have a full existence.*
* *Sovereignty is not given, it is taken.*
* *A nation which makes the final sacrifice for life and freedom does not get beaten.*

DR THOMAS J. BARNARDO (1845-1905) Initiated November 1889 in Shadwell Clerke Lodge No. 1910 in London. Philanthropist and social reformer. Founder of the Barnardo home for orphaned boys.

* *The work to me is everything, and I would throw every rule overboard and send them to the bottom of the sea tomorrow, if I felt there were a more excellent way.*
* *Only disaster can follow divided counsels and opposing wills.*
* *Character is better than ancestry, and personal conduct is of more importance than the highest.*

YASHA BERESINER (1940-) Initiated Lodge of Faith and Friendship No. 7326 London, October 1975. Past Master Quatuor Coronati Lodge of Research No. 2076 1998. Enthusiastic Freemason. International polyglot.

* *Freemasonry to me has been a great and enjoyable game of*

dignified fun. Not unlike Monopoly. I did as the dice dictated without challenging the instructions. I knew that if I did not like the rules, I could not change them, but I could always leave this one and find another game to play.

* *Total mutual tolerance without imposition is the true, maybe the only, secret of the long-standing success of our Craft.*
* *If I was obliged to define Freemasonry with a single word, I would say 'Charity'. Bearing in mind that we speak not merely of charity of the pocket but, maybe more importantly, charity of the heart.*

IRVING BERLIN (1888-1989) Initiated Munn Lodge No. 190 New York and active in the Ancient & Accepted Scottish Rite (Rose Croix) and the Shriners. American composer and songwriter including *White Christmas*.

* *The toughest thing about success is that you have got to keep on being a success.*
* *Life is 10 per cent what you make it, and 90 per cent how you take it.*
* *Our attitudes control our lives. Attitudes are a secret power working twenty-four hours a day, for good or bad. It is of paramount importance that we know how to harness and control this great force.*

SILVIO BERLUSCONI (1936-) Member of the disbanded Propaganda Due (P2) Lodge expelled in 1981 (possibly 1976) by the Grand Orient of Italy. Italian politician and businessman nicknamed *'Il Cavaliere'*. Served three terms as Prime Minister (1994/95, 2001/6 and 2008/11). Controlling shareholder of 'Mediaset'and owner of AC Milan football team.

* *I'm not a traditional politician, and I have a sense of humour. I'll try to soften it and become boring, maybe even very boring, but I'm not sure if I'll be able to.*

* *If I, taking care of everyone's interests, also take care of my own, you can't talk about a conflict of interest.*
* *The political tradition of ancient thought, filtered in Italy by Machiavelli, says one thing clearly: every prince needs allies, and the bigger the responsibility, the more allies he needs.*

SIMÓN BOLÍVAR (1783-1830) Full name: Simón José Antonio de la Santísima Trinidad Bolívar y Palacios Ponte y Blanco. Initiated 1803 Lodge Lautaro, Cadiz, Spain. (This famous Lodge was the mother Lodge of leading South American patriots including José de San Martín, Bernardo O'Higgins, José María Zapiola, Carlos María de Alvear and Mariano Moreno). He received his Master Masons Degree in a Scottish Lodge in Paris in May 1806. Involved with the Knights Templar Order, in 1823 he was appointed Inspector General Honorary, 33rd by the Ancient and Accepted Scottish Rite of Freemasonry (Southern Masonic Jurisdiction) in the United States. Simón Bolívar was a Venezuelan military leader nicknamed 'George Washington of South America' and considered the most influential Latin American soldier and politician in history. He played a key role in Spanish America's successful struggle for independence from the Spanish yoke.

* *Judgement comes from experience, and experience comes from bad judgement.*
* *An ignorant people is the blind instrument of its own destruction.*
* *If my death contributes to the ceasing of the parties and to the consolidation of the union, I shall go down in peace to my tomb.*

JAMES BOSWELL (1740-1795) Raised at Canongate-Kilwinning Lodge, Edinburgh 1759. Came from a family of distinguished Scottish Freemasons. Friend and biographer of Dr Samuel Johnson.

* *A man indeed is not genteel when he gets drunk; but most vices may be committed genteelly; a man may debauch his friend's wife genteelly; he may cheat at cards genteelly.*
* *Claret is the liquor for boys; port, for men; but he who aspires to be a hero must drink brandy. (quoting Johnson)*
* *A companion loves some agreeable qualities which a man may possess, but a friend loves the man himself.*

GENERAL OMAR BRADLEY (1893-1981) Raised in West Point Lodge No. 877 New York State. Second World War American General and Chairman of the US Joint Chiefs of Staff (1949-1953).

* *We have grasped the mystery of the atom and rejected the Sermon on the Mount.*
* *I am convinced that the best service a retired general can perform is to turn in his tongue along with his suit and to mothball his opinions.*
* *Ours is a world of nuclear giants and ethical infants. We know more about war than we know about peace, more about killing than we know about living.*

CHIEF JOSEPH BRANT (1742-1807) An active mason Initiated in Hiram's Cliftonian Lodge No. 417 London in 1776, raised the same year in Lodge No. 417 at the Falcons, Leicester Fields, London. Founding Master of Brantford Lodge No. 31 in 1798 and affiliated to the Barton Lodge, now No. 6, Hamilton, Ontario. Chief Mohawk Thayendanegea served as Principal Chief of the Six Nations Indians. Devoted Christian and a British military officer during the U.S. War of Independence.

* *Indeed it is very hard, when we have let the King's subjects have so much of our lands for so little value.*
* *The Mohawks have on all occasions shown their zeal and loyalty to the Great King; yet they have been very badly treated by his people.*
* *We are tired out in making complaints and getting no redress.*

LUTHER BURBANK (1849-1926) Raised in Santa Rosa Lodge No. 57 (now named Santa Rosa Luther Burbank) California 1921. American horticulturalist famed for the blight-resistant Burbank potato.

* *Heredity is nothing but stored environment.*
* *Flowers always make people better, happier, and more helpful; they are sunshine, food and medicine for the soul.*
* *It is well for people who think to change their minds occasionally in order to keep them clean. For those who do not think, it is best at least to rearrange their prejudices once in a while.*

ROBERT BURNS (1759-1796) Initiated St David's Lodge No. 174 Tarbolton, Ayrshire 1781. Member of several Lodges. Poet Laureate of Lodge No. 2 in Edinburgh. Scottish poet and author of *Auld Lang Syne*, now part of New Year celebrations worldwide.

* *Freedom and Whisky gang thegither!*
* *Don't let the awkward squad fire over me.* (Uttered before dying)
* *Firmness in enduring and exertion is a character I always wish to possess. I have always despised the whining yelp of complaint and cowardly resolve.*

DONALD CAMPBELL (1921-1967) Initiated on 16 February 1953 Grand Master's Lodge No. 1. Son of racing hero Malcolm (see below). On 17 July 1964 broke new world record of 403.1mph at the dry Lake Eyre in South Australia. Only person in history to have held both water and land speed records in the same year. Died 4 January 1967 on Coniston Water in Cumbria attempting a new world record.

* *There is no hope of bailing out of a speedboat racer.*
* *If we have freedom, we have life. Therefore to live, we must love our fellow man, or all will live with the chains of strife.*
* Last recorded words: *Hallo, the bow is up…I'm going…I'm on my back…I've gone. Oh!*

MALCOLM CAMPBELL (1885-1948) Initiated in October 1924 in his own Old Uppinghamian Lodge No. 4227 in Rutland. (Reports that Malcolm Campbell was in fact initiated in Lodge 1870 and was a joining member of the 'closed' Old Uppinghamian Lodge are erroneous.) Active Freemason. World famous speed record breaker. First to reach the 300 miles per hour mark in his celebrated Bluebird at Bonneville Flats, Utah in 1935.

* *Hurry boys, hurry, we have to make a quick change or the hour will be up.*
* *The news comes somewhat late, but I'm glad to hear it nevertheless.*
* *The tyres were scorching hot; in fact I burned my fingers on one.*

GIOVANNI CASANOVA (1725-1798) Real name Jean-Jacques, Chevalier de Seingalt, made a Mason in Lyon, France 1750 en route to Paris where he was raised in the same year. Frequent references to his Masonic activities are to be found in his 12 volume *Mémoires de J. Casanova de Seingalt*. Here he claims to have been arrested in Venice in 1755 for being a Freemason and his apron being used as evidence. Famed libertine, author, spy, diplomat and womaniser.

* *As to the deceit perpetrated upon women, let it pass, for, when love is in the way, men and women as a general rule dupe each other.*
* *For my future I have no concern, and as a true philosopher, I never would have any, for I know not what it may be: as a Christian, on the other hand, faith must believe without discussion, and the stronger it is, the more it keeps silent.*
* *Heart and head are the constituent parts of character; temperament has almost nothing to do with it, and, therefore, character is dependent upon education, and is susceptible of being corrected and improved.*

MARC CHAGALL (1887-1985) Initiated (probably) Lodge at Vitebsk, Belorussia 1912. Russian artist, lived in Paris. Well known for his quasi-Masonic stained glass windows at the Hadassah Hospital Jerusalem.

* *The fingers must be educated; the thumb is born knowing.*
* *All colours are the friends of their neighbours and the lovers of their opposites.*
* *The dignity of the artist lies in his duty of keeping awake the sense of wonder in the world. In this long vigil he often has to vary his methods of stimulation; but in this long vigil he is also himself striving against a continual tendency to sleep.*

WINSTON CHURCHILL (1874-1965) Initiated Studholme Lodge No. 1591 London 1901. Statesman and author. Nobel Prize Winner for Literature 1953.

* *There are two things that are more difficult than making an after-dinner speech: climbing a wall which is leaning toward you and kissing a girl who is leaning away from you.*
* *I am fond of pigs. Dogs look up to us and cats look down on us. Pigs treat us as equals.*
* *We are all worms, but I do believe that I am a glowworm.*

CONFUCIUS (551BC–479BC) Chinese philosopher, *not* a Freemason but should have been one. A man with a Freemason's heart, whose sayings are too important to omit from a book of quotations.

* *I am not bothered by the fact that I am unknown. I am bothered when I do not know others.*
* *The ancient scholars studied for their own improvement. Modern scholars study to impress others.*
* *When a person should be spoken with, and you don't speak with them, you lose them. When a person shouldn't be spoken with and you speak to them, you waste your breath. The wise do not lose people, nor do they waste their breath.*

TOMMY COOPER (1921-1984) Initiated December 1952 St Margaret's Westminster Lodge No. 4518 London. Much loved and popular Welsh magician and comedian readily recognisable by his red fez.

* *A blind bloke walks into a shop with a guide dog. He picks the dog up and starts swinging it around his head. Alarmed, a shop assistant calls out: 'Can I help, sir?' 'No thanks,' says the blind bloke. 'Just looking.'*
* *A woman tells her doctor, 'I've got a bad back.' The doctor says, 'It's old age.' The woman says, 'I want a second opinion.' The doctor replies: 'Okay – you're ugly as well.'*
* *You know, somebody actually complimented me on my driving today. They left a little note on the windscreen. It said 'Parking Fine'.*

JIM DAVIDSON (1953-) Initiated 1991 in Chelsea Lodge No. 3098, London from which he resigned in July 2002. Also the first Worshipful Master of British Forces Foundation Lodge No. 9725. Controversial British comedian, actor and television presenter.

* *You'd make a good burglar – your arse would rub your footprints out.*

* *I went into the bar and asked for a Bloody Mary and they thought I was being blasphemous.*
* *If I've offended anyone, I will apologise, but in the 70s I didn't have a lot to apologise for. Maybe all the audience that came to see me and made me rich and famous should apologise to their ethnic neighbours.*

JACK DEMPSEY (1895-1983) Member of Kenwood Lodge No. 800 Chicago. American world heavyweight boxing champion (1919) which he retained for seven years.

* *A champion is someone who gets up when he can't.*
* *I was a pretty good fighter. But it was the writers who made me great.*
* *Honey, I just forgot to duck. (To his wife, on losing the world heavyweight title)*

ARTHUR CONAN DOYLE (1859-1930) Raised in Phoenix Lodge No. 257 Portsmouth, England 1893. English novelist and famed creator of Sherlock Holmes who, with his faithful Dr Watson, appeared in three novels and 56 short stories. (Sherlock Holmes himself was not a Mason, though he knew an awful lot about it).

* *A man should keep his little brain attic stocked with all the furniture that he is likely to use, and the rest he can put away in the lumber room of his library, where he can get it if he wants it.*
* *It is quite a three-pipe problem.*
* *London, that great cesspool into which all the loungers and idlers of the Empire are irresistibly drained.*

RICHARD DREYFUSS (1947-) Made a Mason 'at sight' at the Scottish Rite Temple in Washington, December 2011. The ceremony included 1st to the 3rd Degree of the Craft followed by the other degrees of the Ancient & Accepted Rite up to, and including, the 32nd. American film and television star. Academy award winner in 1977.

* *Happiness has a bad rap. People say it shouldn't be your goal in life. Oh, yes it should.*
* *I don't know what it's like for most actors, but really clearly for myself acting has always been the fulfilment of personal fantasies. It isn't just art, it's about being a person I've always wanted to be. Being in a situation, or being a hero.*
* *Living is the process of going from complete certainty to complete ignorance.*

DUKE OF EDINBURGH (1921-) Prince Philip, Duke of Edinburgh, was initiated in Navy Lodge No. 2612, London and though he has not been active, he has continued to pay his Lodge dues to date. Prince Philip is the Queen's husband, the Royal consort to Queen Elizabeth II.

* *Everybody was saying we must have more leisure. Now they are complaining they are unemployed.*
* *I don't think a prostitute is more moral than a wife, but they are doing the same thing.*
* *When a man opens a car door for his wife, it's either a new car or a new wife.*

KING EDWARD VII (1841-1910) Albert Edward, Prince of Wales, a popular Grand Master from 1874 to the year of his coronation in 1901. Initiated in Stockholm, Sweden by King Charles XV in 1868. Received Ancient and Accepted Rite degrees in 1875. He made Freemasonry a fashionable pursuit in England. When crowned he became King of the United Kingdom and the British Dominions and Emperor of India.

* *One not only drinks the wine, one smells it, observes it, tastes it, sips it and one talks about it.*
* *I never can, or shall, look at him without a shudder.* (Queen Victoria who had a low opinion of her eldest son Edward)
* *I believe the emperor of Germany hates me.*

KING EDWARD VIII (1894-1972) Provincial Grand Master for Surrey, Grand Master of the UGLE 1936, the year of his abdication after less than one year's reign. He abdicated to marry Mrs Simpson and was created the Duke of Windsor.

* *I wanted to be an up-to-date king. But I didn't have much time.*
* *Of course, I do have a slight advantage over the rest of you. It helps in a pinch to be able to remind your bride that you gave up a throne for her.*
* *The thing that impresses me most about America is the way parents obey their children.*

W. C. FIELDS (1880-1946) Member of E Coppee Mitchell Lodge No. 605, Philadelphia USA. William Claude Fields was an American comedian famed for his intolerance, eccentricity and misogynist approach to life.

* *We frequently hear of people dying from too much drinking. That this happens is a matter of record. But the blame almost always is placed on whisky. Why this should be I never could understand. You can die from drinking too much of anything – coffee, water, milk, soft drinks and all such stuff as that. And so long as the presence of death lurks with anyone who goes through the simple act of swallowing, I will make mine whiskey.*
* *Hell, I never vote for anybody. I always vote against.*
* *It was a woman who drove me to drink – and, you know, I never even thanked her.*

ALEXANDER FLEMING (1881-1955) Initiated in Sancta Maria Lodge No. 2682, London 1909. Member of many Lodges and Grand Officer of the UGLE. Scottish bacteriologist, discoverer of penicillin (1928) and winner of the Nobel Prize for Medicine in 1945.

* *A good gulp of hot whisky at bedtime – it's not very scientific but it helps.*
* *I have been trying to point out that in our lives chance may have an astonishing influence and, if I may offer advice to the young laboratory worker, it would be this – never to neglect an extraordinary appearance or happening.*
* *It is the lone worker who makes the first advance in a subject; the details may be worked out by a team, but the prime idea is due to enterprise, thought, and perception of an individual.*

HENRY FORD (1863-1947) Raised in Palestine Lodge No. 357 Detroit, Michigan in November 1894. Honorary member of Zion Lodge 1 (Michigan). Received the 33rd degree A&AR September 1940. American industrialist and philanthropist, creator, in 1903, of the Ford Motor Company.

* *An idealist is a person who helps other people to be prosperous.*
* *History is more or less bunk. It's tradition. We don't want tradition. We want to live in the present and the only history that is worth a tinker's dam is the history we made today.*
* *All Fords are exactly alike, but no two men are just alike. Every new life is a new thing under the sun; there has never been anything just like it before, never will be again. A young man ought to get that idea about himself; he should look for the single spark of individuality that makes him different from other folks, and develop that for all he is worth. Society and schools may try to iron it out of him; their tendency is to put it all in the same mould, but I say don't let that spark be lost; it is your only real claim to importance.*

BENJAMIN FRANKLIN (1706-1790) Initiated St John's Lodge Philadelphia, Pennsylvania 1731. Grand Master, Grand Lodge of Pennsylvania (1734). Very active American Freemason. Statesman, inventor, scientist and philosopher. Signatory to the Declaration of Independence.

* *There is a difference between imitating a good man and counterfeiting him.*
* *The greatest monarch on the proudest throne is obliged to sit upon his own arse.*
* *There are three faithful friends: an old wife, and old dog, and ready money.*

GIUSEPPE GARIBALDI (1807-1882) Initiated in Lodge L'Ami de la Patrie, Montevideo, Uruguay (Grand Orient of France) 1844. Famously, in a complex and muddled history, never passed or raised before becoming Grand Master of the Grand Orient in Turin and Sovereign Grand Commander of the Supreme Council of the Ancient and Accepted Scottish Rite (Italy).

* *Bacchus has drowned more men than Neptune.*
* *I offer neither pay, nor quarters, nor food; I offer only hunger, thirst, forced marches, battles and death. Let him who loves his country with his heart, and not merely with his lips, follow me.*
* *To this wonderful page in our country's history another more glorious still will be added, and the slave shall show at last to his free brothers a sharpened sword forged from the links of his fetters.*

KING GEORGE VI (1895-1952) Initiated Naval Lodge No. 2612 1919. Succeeded to the throne under controversial circumstances of his brother's abdication in 1936, Grand Master of Scotland 1936. 1938 Past Grand Master of the UGLE. Famously, he personally installed three Grand Masters.

* *Abroad is bloody.*
* *The highest of distinctions is service to others.*
* *From the film 'The King's Speech' (2010)*
  Lionel Logue: *What was your earliest memory?*
  King George VI: *I'm not…here to discuss…personal matters.*
  Lionel Logue: *Why are you here then?*
  King George VI: *Because I bloody well stammer!*
  Lionel Logue: *Do you know any jokes?*
  King George VI: *…Timing isn't my strong suit.*

EDWARD GIBBON (1737-1794) Initiated December 1774, Lodge of Friendship No. 3 in London. English historian and Member of Parliament. Author of the voluminous *The History of the Decline and Fall of the Roman Empire*.

* *A heart to resolve, a head to contrive, and a hand to execute.*
* *Beauty is an outward gift which is seldom despised, except by those to whom it has been refused.*
* *Conversation enriches the understanding, but solitude is the school of genius.*

SIR WILLIAM GILBERT (1836-1911) Of Gilbert and Sullivan fame. Raised in St Machar Lodge No. 54 Aberdeen, Scotland. English playwright and lyricist partnering Sir Arthur Sullivan (also a Freemason) who wrote the music for the world famed 'Savoy Operas'. Titles such as *The Mikado*, *Pirates of Penzance*, etc, are household names.

* *When everyone is somebody, then no one is anybody.*
  (The Gondoliers)
* *Things are seldom what they seem,*
  skimmed milk masquerades as cream. (HMS Pinafore)
* *I can trace my ancestry back to a protoplasmal primordial*
  atomic globule.
  Consequently, my family pride is something inconceivable.
  I can't help it. I was born sneering. (The Mikado)

JOHANN WOLFGANG GOETHE (1749-1832) Initiated
in Amalia Lodge in Weimar, Germany on 23 June 1780 under
the then prevalent Rite of Strict Observance. German novelist,
scientist and poet of the Romantic School, which he instituted.
Famed for many classical literary works including *Faust*. He also
wrote some Masonic pieces.

* *From desire I plunge to its fulfilment, where I long once more*
  for fulfilment.
* *If a man thinks about his physical or moral state, he usually*
  discovers that he is ill.
* *A clever man commits no minor blunders.*

DOUGLAS, FIRST EARL HAIG (1861-1928) Initiated Elgin
Lodge No. 91 St Leven, Scotland in 1881. Scottish Field Marshall
and Commander in Chief in France in 1916. Closely associated
with the Battle of the Somme.

* *A very weak minded fellow, I am afraid, and, like the feather*
  pillow, bears the marks of the last person who has sat on him.
* *The idea that a war can be won by standing on the defensive and*
  waiting for the enemy to attack is a dangerous fallacy, which owes
  its inception to the desire to evade the price of victory.
* *Once the mass of the defending infantry become possessed of low*
  moral, the battle is as good as lost.

OLIVER HARDY (1892-1957) Member (probably initiated in) Solomon Lodge No. 20 Jacksonville, Florida, USA. American actor and comedian in world-famed partnership with English comedian Stan Laurel. Hardy's ashes were interred in the Masonic Garden of Valhalla Memorial Park in North Hollywood.

* *Here's another fine mess you've gotten me into.*
* *We never see ourselves as others see us.*
* *Despite rumours to the contrary, Oliver Hardy did not die from obesity. Dieting on doctor's orders, he took off too much weight too fast, going from more than 300 pounds to 150 in a matter of a few weeks. He so weakened his constitution as to cause his eventual illness and death in 1957*

HARRY HOUDINI (1874-1926) Real name Erich Weiss. Made a Mason in New York, St Cecile Lodge No 568 'the Lodge of the Arts' in 1923. American magician, escapologist and author. Al Jolson, Louis B. Mayer, Vincent Lopez and Paul Whiteman are other famous entertainers who were members of the Lodge.

* *Another method of eating burning coals employs small balls of burned cotton in a dish of burning alcohol.*
* *How the early priests came into possession of these secrets does not appear, and if there were ever any records of this kind the Church would hardly allow them to become public.*
* *The great day of the Fire-eater – or, should I say, the day of the great Fire-eater – has passed.*

ROBERT HOUGHWOUT JACKSON (1892-1954) Listed as one of the 96 United States Supreme Court Justices who were Freemasons, Jackson was the United States Attorney General (1940-1941) and an Associate Justice of the United States Supreme Court (1941-1954). He was also the chief United States prosecutor at the Nuremberg Trials. Exceptionally, he was appointed to the Supreme Court though he did not graduate from any law school.

* *Any lawyer worth his salt will tell the suspect in no uncertain terms to make no statement to the police under any circumstances.*
* *We [in the Supreme Court] are not final because we are infallible, but we are infallible only because we are final.*
* *When the Supreme Court moved to Washington in 1800, it was provided with no books, which probably accounts for the high quality of early opinions.*

DOUGLAS JERROLD (1803-1857) Initiated Bank of England Lodge No. 329 in 1831. English author and playwright closely associated with the satirical magazine *Punch*.

* *Australia is so kind that, just tickle her with a hoe, she laughs with a harvest.*
* *If an earthquake was to engulf England tomorrow, the English would manage to meet and dine somewhere among the rubbish, just to celebrate the event.*
* *He is one of those wise philanthropists who in a time of famine would vote for nothing but a supply of toothpicks.*

RUDYARD KIPLING (1865-1936) Initiated Hope & Esperance Lodge No. 782 Lahore, India. English author. Nobel Prize Winner for Literature 1907.

* *Think what could have been done by Masonry, through Masonry, for the entire world.*
* *A woman's guess is much more accurate than a man's certainty.*
* *Borrow trouble for yourself, if that's your nature, but don't lend it to your neighbours.*

HORATIO KITCHENER (1850-1916) Initiated in Cairo, Egypt at La Concordia Lodge No. 1226, English constitution. Dedicated high-ranking Freemason, Irish born highly honoured and decorated Field Marshal. Soldier and politician gained immortality through the famous First World War recruiting poster 'Your Country Needs You'.

* *Margot Asquith said of Lord Kitchener: 'If Kitchener is not a*
  great man, he is,
  at least, a great poster.'
* *Kitchener never loved a woman. Rumours of his being*
  a homosexual have persisted. Evidence supposedly lies in
  Kitchener's friendship with Captain Oswald Fitzgerald, his
  aide-de-camp and 'constant and inseparable Companion'. They
  remained close friends and died together on the voyage to Russia.
  He also was known to be surrounded – since his time in Egypt
  in 1892 – by young and eager unmarried officers nicknamed
  'Kitchener's band of boys'. The Guardian *newspaper, as recently*
  as 21 February 2005, remarked that Kitchener 'had the failing
  acquired by most of the Egyptian officers, a taste for buggery'.
* *Lord Kitchener's contribution to the home front is reflected in*
  the 'Kitchener stitch'. It refers to the knitted sock patterns at the
  time which rubbed uncomfortably against the toes. British and
  American women were prompted by Kitchener to knit a seamless
  sock pattern still in use today and attributed to him.

MARQUIS DE LAFAYETTE (1757-1834) Initiated possibly in Paris or, more likely, in the USA in the presence of George Washington. He was received with distinguished honours by the Grand Lodge of Pennsylvania in 1826. French military officer who served as a General in the American Revolutionary War and a leader of the *Garde Nationale* during the French Revolution.

* *Humanity has won its battle. Liberty now has a country.*
* *If the liberties of the American people are ever destroyed, they will fall by the hands of the clergy.*
* *True republicanism is the sovereignty of the people. There are natural and imprescriptible rights which an entire nation has no right to violate.*

GOTTHOLD E. LESSING (1729-1781) Initiated Zu den Drei Goldenen Rosen Lodge, Hamburg 1771. German dramatist known for Masonic poems and the Masonic dialogue *Ernst und Falk*.

* *He who doesn't lose his wits over certain things has no wits to lose.*
* *A heretic is a man who sees with his own eyes.*
* *It is not the truth that a man possesses, or believes that he possesses, but the earnest effort which he puts forward to reach the truth, which constitutes the worth of a man.*

CHARLES LINDBERGH (1902-1974) Initiated in 1926 Keystone Lodge No. 243, St Louis, Missouri. American aviator who made the first non-stop transatlantic flight from New York to Paris. His plane was the *Spirit of St Louis* and bore the Masonic insignia.

* *It is the greatest shot of adrenaline to be doing what you have wanted to do so badly. You almost feel like you could fly without the plane.*
* *I owned the world that hour as I rode over it. Free of the earth, free of the mountains, free of the clouds, but how inseparably I was bound to them.*
* *If I had to choose, I would rather have birds than airplanes.*

DOUGLAS MacARTHUR (1880-1964) Made a Mason 'at sight' by the Grand Master of the Grand Lodge of the Philippines in January 1936 and affiliated to Manila Lodge No. 1. In the same year he received his 32nd degree of the A&AR also in Manila. Legendary American soldier who served as Chief of Staff in World War 1 and as a 5-star General and Allied Supreme Commander in World War 2.

* *A general is just as good or just as bad as the troops under his command make him.*
* *Build me a son, O Lord, who will be strong enough to know when he is weak, and brave enough to face himself when he is afraid, one who will be proud and unbending in honest defeat, and humble and gentle in victory.*
* *Age wrinkles the body. Quitting wrinkles the soul.*

JAN MASARYK (1886-1948) Initiated Jan Amos Komensky Lodge No. 1, Prague. Czechoslovak statesman and patriot.

* *Dictators are rulers who always look good until the last ten minutes.*

ANDREW MELLON (1855-1937) Made Mason 'at sight', Pittsburgh 1928. American banker and industrialist, art collector and philanthropist.

* *Gentlemen prefer bonds.*
* *Give tax breaks to large corporations, so that money can trickle down to the general public, in the form of extra jobs.*
* *Liquidate labour, liquidate stocks, liquidate farmers.*

BOB MONKHOUSE (1928-2003) Member of Chelsea Lodge No. 3098. English actor, comedian, memory man and television presenter.

* *They laughed when I said I was going to be a comedian. Well, they're not laughing now, are they.*
* *If you don't go to other people's funerals, they won't go to yours.*
* *I can still enjoy sex at 74 – I live at 75, so it's no distance.*

WOLFGANG AMADEUS MOZART (1756-1791) Initiated Lodge Zur Wohltätigkeit (Benevolence), Vienna 1784. Austrian classical composer. *The Magic Flute* is famed for its Masonic connotations.

* *I write as a sow piddles.*
* *To talk well and elegantly is a very great art, but an equally great one is to know the right moment to stop.*
* *Music, even in situations of the greatest horror, should never be painful to the ear but should flatter and charm it, and thereby always remain music.*

DANIEL O'CONNELL (1775-1847) Raised in 1797 and served as Master in 1800 of Lodge No. 189, Dublin. Also member of Lodge No. 13 in Limerick. Irish catholic lawyer, politician and patriot nicknamed 'The Liberator'. Lord Mayor of Dublin in 1841.

* *The Englishman has all the qualities of a poker, except its occasional warmth.*
* *Peel's smile: like a silver plate on a coffin.*
* *Nothing is politically right which is morally wrong.*

JOE PASQUALE (1961-) Initiated Chelsea Lodge No. 3098 May 2005. English comedian and television presenter, renowned for his extremely high-pitched voice.

* *If you look like your passport photo you're too ill to travel.*
* *I've been in the business for 20 years, then I come on this show*

(TV reality), *sit on my arse, eat crap, jump out of an aeroplane – and now everyone wants to talk about me.*

* *Winning was like going on a crap holiday and coming back like Elvis.* (on being crowned 'King of the Jungle' in the TV show I'm a Celebrity…*Get Me Out of Here*)

ALEXANDER POPE (1688-1744) Thought to be a member of Lodge No. 16 held at *The Goat*, a tavern at the foot of The Haymarket in London also frequented by Jonathan Swift, his friend. Quintessential English poet and satirist.

* *Who shall decide when Doctors disagree?*
* *As some to church repair,*
Not for the doctrine, but the music there.
* *It is with narrow-souled people as with narrow-necked bottles: the less they have in them, the more noise they make in pouring it out.*

JOHANN PAUL RICHTER (1763-1825) Member of Lodge Pforte zum Tempel des Lichts, Hof, Germany. Popular German author and novelist.

* *Sleep, riches and health, to be truly enjoyed, must be interrupted.*
* *A variety of nothing is superior to a monotony of something.*
* *Humanity is never so beautiful as when praying for forgiveness, or else forgiving another.*

FRANKLIN DELANO ROOSEVELT (1882-1945) Initiated October 1911 in Holland Lodge No. 8, New York City. Also a member of the Scottish Rite. Active and honorary member of other Lodges. 32nd President of the USA (1932-1945). In 1921 suffered from a polio attack and was thereafter paralysed from the waist down and later confined to a wheelchair.

* *A conservative is a man with two perfectly good legs who, however, has never learned how to walk forward.*
* *Be sincere; be brief; be seated.*
* *A nation that destroys its soils destroys itself. Forests are the lungs of our land, purifying the air and giving fresh strength to our people.*

THEODORE ROOSEVELT (1858-1919) Initiated January 1801 Matinecock Lodge No. 806, Oyster Bay, New York State. Honorary and active member of other Lodges. 26th President of the USA (1901-1909).

* *A man who has never gone to school may steal from a freight car; but if he has a university education, he may steal the whole railroad.*
* *A thorough knowledge of the Bible is worth more than a college education.*
* *A typical vice of American politics is the avoidance of saying anything real on real issues.*

NATHAN MAYER ROTHSCHILD (1777-1836) Member of Emulation Lodge No. 21. English (and German) financier and founder of the English branch of the Rothschild 'empire'.

* *It isn't enough for you to love money – it is also necessary that money should love you.*
* *We are like the mechanism of a watch: each part is essential.*
* *As long as a house is like yours, and as long as you work together with your brothers, not a house in the world will be able to compete with you, to cause you harm or to take advantage of you, for together you can undertake and perform more than any house in the world.*

WALTER SCOTT (1771-1832) Initiated, passed and raised Saint David Lodge No. 36, Edinburgh, March 1801. Prolific Scottish poet and novelist.

* *A lawyer without history or literature is a mechanic, a mere working mason; if he possesses some knowledge of these, he may venture to call himself an architect.*
* *The ae half of the warld thinks the tither daft.*
* *A rusty nail placed near a faithful compass will sway it from the truth, and wreck the argosy.*

PETER SELLERS (1925-1980) Initiated 16 July 1948, Chelsea Lodge No. 3098, London. English actor and comedian.

* *Conversation is like a television set on a honeymoon… unnecessary.*
* *I feel ghostly unreal until I become somebody else again on the screen.*
* *There is no me. I do not exist. There used to be a me but I had it surgically removed.*

JEAN SIBELIUS (1865-1957) Initiated in 1922 in Suomi Lodge No. 1 Helsinki, Finland and a founding member of the Grand Lodge of Finland. Greatest of Scandinavian composers. Created many compositions for Masonic occasions.

* *If the critics were always right, we should be in deep trouble… pay no attention to what the critics say; no statue has ever been put up to a critic.*

HENRI BEYLE STENDHAL (1783-1842) Inducted into Sainte Caroline Lodge, Paris in 1806. French novelist.

* *The first qualification for a historian is to have no ability to invent.*

* *Since I am a man, my heart is three or four times less sensitive, because I have three or four times as much power of reason and experience of the world – a thing which you women call hard-heartedness.*
* *As a man, I can take refuge in having mistresses. The more of them I have, and the greater the scandal, the more I acquire reputation and brilliance in society.*

JONATHAN SWIFT (1667-1745) Believed to have been a member of Lodge No. 16 that met at a tavern at the foot of The Haymarket in London. Irish satirist and poet, author of *Gulliver's Travels*.

* *Satire is a sort of glass (mirror), wherein beholders do generally discover everybody's face but their own.*
* *Walls have tongues and hedges have ears.*
* *What some invent, the rest enlarge.*

JAMES THOMSON (1700-1748) Initiated in the Lodge meeting at The Old Man's Coffee House, London 1737. Scottish poet.

* *Here lies a man that never lived,*
  Yet still from death was flying;
  Who, if not sick, was never well;
  And died – for fear of dying!
* *For life is but a dream whose shapes return, some frequently, some seldom, some by night and some by day.*
* *I know no subject more elevating, more amazing, more ready to the poetical enthusiasm, the philosophical reflection, and the moral sentiment than the works of nature. Where can we meet such variety, such beauty, such magnificence?*

ANTHONY TROLLOPE (1815-1882) Initiated Banghar Lodge No. 306, Ireland 1841. English political novelist.

* *He must have known me had he seen me as he was wont to see me, for he was in the habit of flogging me constantly. Perhaps he did not recognise me by my face.*
* *I doubt whether any girl would be satisfied with her lover's mind if she knew the whole of it.*
* *There is no villainy to which education cannot reconcile us.*

HARRY S. TRUMAN (1884-1972) Belton Lodge No. 450, Belton, Missouri. Grand Master of Missouri, 1940-1941. 33rd President of the United States of America (1945–1953).

* *A politician is a man who understands government. A statesman is a politician who's been dead for 15 years.*
* *I have found the best way to give advice to your children is to find out what they want and then advise them to do it.*
* *If you cannot convince them, confuse them.*

MARK TWAIN (1835-1910) Real name Samuel Langhorne Clemens. Member of Polar Star Lodge No. 79 St. Louis, Missouri. (Suspended for non-payment of dues and later reinstated 24 April 1867.)

* *It usually takes more than three weeks to prepare a good impromptu speech.*
* *A round man cannot be expected to fit in a square hole right away. He must have time to modify his shape.*
* *Anger is an acid that can do more harm to the vessel in which it is stored than to anything on which it is poured.*

FRANÇOIS MARIE AROUET DE VOLTAIRE (1694-1778)
Initiated 7 April 1778 in the Paris Lodge *Les Neuf Sœurs*, famed for its support for the American Revolution. Voltaire was escorted by Benjamin Franklin. French philosopher and author.

* *A multitude of laws in a country is like a great number of physicians, a sign of weakness and malady.*
* *England has forty-two religions and only two sauces.*
* *Never having been able to succeed in the world, he took his revenge by speaking ill of it.*

GEORGE WASHINGTON (1732-1799) Initiated November 1752 in the Lodge at Fredericksburg in Virginia. First President and hero of the Independence of the United States of America.

* *Associate yourself with men of good quality if you esteem your own reputation. It is better to be alone than in bad company.*
* *Discipline is the soul of an army. It makes small numbers formidable, procures success to the weak, and esteem to all.*
* *A slender acquaintance with the world must convince every man that actions, not words, are the true criterion of the attachment of friends.*

ARTHUR DUKE OF WELLINGTON (WELLESLEY) (1769-1852) Initiated Trim Lodge No. 494, Ireland, December 1790. He came from a family of high ranking Masons. His father and brother were Grand Masters of the Grand Lodge of Ireland. Statesman and soldier known as 'The Iron Duke'.

* *Be discreet in all things, and so render it unnecessary to be mysterious.*
* *Possible? Is anything impossible? Read the newspapers!*
* *I don't know what effect these men will have upon the enemy, but, by God, they terrify me.*

OSCAR WILDE (1854-1900) Initiated Apollo Lodge No. 357, Oxford 1875. Fascinated by orders beyond the Craft especially Rose Croix. Acclaimed Irish dramatist and wit.

* *Moderation is a fatal thing. Enough is as bad as a meal. More than enough is as good as a feast.*
* *To be good is to be in harmony with oneself. Discord is to be forced to be in harmony with others.*
* *Ah, well then, I shall have to die the way I lived...beyond my means.*
  (At his death-bed, on being told of the high fee for surgery)

SIR CHRISTOPHER WREN (1632-1723) The 2011 Prestonian Lecture on Christopher Wren by Bro James Campbell is a persuasive argument in favour of Wren having been a Freemason in the years preceding the formation of Grand Lodge of England in 1717. The main evidence states that Wren was 'adopted' on 18 May 1691 as a Freemason and was later to become a member and Master of Antiquity Lodge No. 2. Acclaimed English architect of major works in the 1670s and 1680s including St Paul's Cathedral, completed 1711. Wren was President of the Royal Society in 1680.

* *I am going to dine with some men.*
  If anybody calls,
  Say I am designing St Paul's.
  [Short poem penned in 1905 by Edmund Clerihew Bentley (1875–1956)]
* *An apocryphal story relates to Wren's design of the King's House at Newmarket, in which Charles II, who was over six feet tall, complained about the low ceilings. Wren, who was not so tall, replied that 'they were high enough', at which the king crouched down until he was on a level with his surveyor and strutted about saying, 'Ay, Ay, Sir Christopher, I think they are high enough.'*

* *Clever men, like Christopher Wren,*
  Only occur just now and then,
  No one expects in perpetuity
  Architects of this ingenuity,
  No, never a cleverer dipped his pen
  Than clever Sir Christopher – Christopher Wren.
  (Hugh Chesterman)

APPENDIX A

Global Glossary of Proverbs

Africa
* *When elephants fight it is the grass that suffers.*
* *All would live long, but none would be old.*
* *The African race is a rubber ball. The harder you dash it to the ground, the higher it will rise.*

Albania
* *After shaking hands with a Greek, count your fingers.*

America
* *America is a vast conspiracy to make you happy.*
* *Employ thy time well if thou meanest to get leisure.*
* *Good fences make good neighbours.*

American Indian
* *Listen or thy tongue will keep thee deaf.*
* *Never criticise a man until you've walked a mile in his moccasins.*
* *After dark all cats are leopards.*

Arab
* *Throw a lucky man into the sea, and he will come up with a fish in his mouth.*
* *The sinning is the best part of repentance.*
* *After lunch, rest; after dinner, walk a mile.*

Australian Aboriginal
* *Hypocrite – mouth one way, belly 'nother way.*

Belgium
* *Experience is the comb that Nature gives us when we are bald.*

* *Don't make use of another's mouth unless it has been lent to you.*

Bible (Proverbs)
* *As cold waters to a thirsty soul, so is good news from a far country.*
* *Like a lame man's legs that hang limp is a proverb in the mouth of a fool.*
* *As a dog returneth to his vomit, so a fool returneth to his folly.*

Bulgaria
* *Seize the opportunity by the beard, for it is bald behind.*
* *God promises a safe landing but not a calm passage.*
* *A tree falls the way it leans.*

Burma
* *Beware of a man's shadow and a bee's sting.*
* *If you take big paces you leave big spaces.*

China
* *If heaven made him, earth can find some use for him.*
* *One dog barks at something, the rest bark at him.*
* *To be uncertain is to be uncomfortable, but to be certain is to be ridiculous.*

Colombia
* *He who must die must die in the dark, even though he sells candles.*

Czechoslovakia
* *When you buy, use your eyes and your mind…not your ears.*
* *The big thieves hang the little ones.*
* *Do not protect yourself by a fence, but rather by your friends.*

Denmark
* *Bad is never good until worse happens.*
* *Children are a poor man's wealth.*
* *The dog's kennel is not the place to keep a sausage.*

England
* *A Scotch mist may wet an Englishman to the skin.*
* *Affectation is a greater enemy to the face than smallpox.*
* *We are usually the best men when in the worst health.*

Estonia
* *One woman never praises another.*

Ethiopia
* *When spiders unite they can tie down a lion.*
* *A close friend can become a close enemy.*

France
* *He who can lick can bite.*
* *The price spoils the pleasure.*
* *The worst is not always certain but it's very likely.*

Germany
* *God gives the nuts, but he does not crack them.*
* *Old birds are hard to pluck.*
* *The eyes believe themselves; the ears believe other people.*

Greece
* *Think with the wise, but talk with the vulgar.*
* *All things good to know are difficult to learn.*
* *The beginning is the half of every action.*

Haiti
* *If work were good for you, the rich would leave none for the poor.*
* *If you want your eggs hatched, sit on them yourself.*
* *A monkey never thinks her baby's ugly.*

Hindu
* *An arch never sleeps.*
* *If you ask the hungry man how much is two and two, he replies four loaves.*

* *Dictators ride to and fro upon tigers from which they dare not dismount.*

Holland
* *God does not pay weekly, but he pays at the end.*
* *A handful of patience is worth more than a bushel of brains.*
* *God made the ocean, but the Dutch made Holland.*

Hottentot (South Africa)
* *Good is when I steal other people's wives and cattle; bad is when they steal mine.*
* *An indecent mind is a perpetual feast.*

Hungary
* *A loan though old is not a gift.*
* *A prudent man does not make the goat his gardener.*
* *An ox remains an ox, even if driven to Vienna.*

India
* *Call on God, but row away from the rocks.*
* *Only mad dogs and Englishmen go out in the noonday sun.*
* *When an elephant is in trouble even a frog will kick him.*

Indonesia (Bali)
* *Goodness shouts. Evil whispers.*

Ireland
* *Every invalid is a physician.*
* *Money swore an oath that nobody who did not love it should ever have it.*
* *A dimple in the chin, a devil within.*

Italy
* *He that jokes confesses.*
* *Below the navel there is neither religion nor truth.*
* *Since the house is on fire we might as well warm ourselves.*

Jamaica
* *No call alligator long mouth till you pass him.*
* *The jay bird don't rob his own nest.*

Japan
* *The go-between wears out a thousand sandals.*
* *The nail that sticks out is hammered down.*
* *Life without endeavour is like entering a jewel-mine and coming out with empty hands.*

Kenya
* *You may laugh at a friend's roof; don't laugh at his sleeping accommodation.*
* *He who does not know one thing knows another.*

Korea
* *Where there are no tigers, a wildcat is very self-important.*
* *Power lasts ten years; influence not more than a hundred.*

Kurdistan
* *Do not throw the arrow which will return against you.*

Lancashire
* *Shake a bridle over a Yorkshireman's grave, and he'll rise and steal a horse.*

Latvia
* *A smiling face is half the meal.*

Lebanon
* *Hygiene is two thirds of health.*

Libya
* *He who searches for pearls should not sleep.*

Lithuania
* *God gave teeth; he will give bread.*

Macedonia
* *In the kingdom of the blind the one-eyed are kings.*

Malaysia
* *Don't think there are no crocodiles because the water is calm.*
* *Though a tree grow ever so high, the falling leaves return to the ground.*
* *Trumpet in a herd of elephants; crow in the company of cocks; bleat in a flock of goats.*

Morocco
* *None but a mule deserves his family.*

New Zealand (Maori)
* *Turn your face to the sun and the shadows fall behind you.*

Nigeria
* *When the mouse laughs at the cat there's a hole nearby.*
* *What you give you get, ten times over.*
* *Rain beats a leopard's skin, but it does not wash off the spots.*

Norway
* *Not all keys hang from one girdle.*
* *Old habits have deep roots.*
* *He who follows the river comes at last to the sea.*

Persia
* *If fortune turns against you, even jelly breaks your tooth.*
* *The blind man is laughing at the bald head.*
* *He who wants a rose must respect the thorn.*

Philippines
* *Don't empty the water jar until the rain falls.*

Poland

* *Fish, to taste right, must swim three times – in water, in butter and in wine.*
* *The greater love is a mother's; then comes a dog's; then a sweetheart's.*
* *The woman cries before the wedding and the man after.*

Portugal

* *Visits always give pleasure – if not the arrival, the departure.*
* *The dog wags his tail, not for you, but for your bread.*
* *A house without a dog or a cat is the house of a scoundrel.*

Romania

* *Abundance, like want, ruins many.*
* *Adversity makes a man wise, not rich.*
* *An ass is but an ass, though laden with gold.*

Rome (Ancient)

* *All roads lead to Rome.*
* *Be on your guard against a silent dog and still water.*
* *By learning you will teach; by teaching you will learn.*

Russia

* *Don't buy the house; buy the neighbourhood.*
* *Russia is the only country in the world you can be homesick for while you are still in it.*
* *The rich would have to eat money, but luckily the poor provide food.*

Scotland

* *The Devil's boots don't creak.*
* *What may be done at any time will be done at no time.*
* *Be happy while you're living, for you're a long time dead.*

Siberia

* *June's too soon, July's too late – for summer.*

Slovakia

* Don't shake the tree when the pears fall off themselves.

Slovenia

* All roads do not lead to Rome.
* Speak the truth, but leave immediately after.

Spain

* You can't have more bugs than a blanketful.
* Don't offer me advice, give me money.
* Drink nothing without seeing it; sign nothing without reading it.

Sweden

* The afternoon knows what the morning never suspected.
* Don't let your sorrow come higher than your knees.
* Don't throw away the old bucket until you know whether the new one holds water.

Switzerland

* When one shuts one eye, one does not hear everything.
* The night rinses what the day has soaped.

Talmud (Old Testament)

* The deeper the sorrow the less tongue it hath.
* Beware of too much laughter, for it deadens the mind and produces oblivion.
* He that gives should never remember; he that receives should never forget.

Tibet

* Goodness speaks in a whisper; evil shouts.

Tonga

* Friendship is a furrow in the sand.

Turkey

*   *Remain hungry but do not start begging.*
*   *A heart in love with beauty never grows old.*
*   *Measure a thousand times and cut once.*

Ukraine

*   *The church is near, but the way is icy. The tavern is far, but I will walk carefully.*
*   *Love tells us many things that are not so.*

Venezuela

*   *There is nothing hidden between Heaven and Earth.*

Wales

*   *Three things it is best to avoid a strange dog, a flood, and a man who thinks he is wise.*
*   *A spoon does not know the taste of soup, nor a learned fool the taste of wisdom.*
*   *Have a horse of your own and then you may borrow another's.*

Yiddish

*   *A man should live if only to satisfy his curiosity.*
*   *A wise man hears one word and understands two.*
*   *If rich people could hire other people to die for them, the poor could make a wonderful living.*

Yugoslavia

*   *Complain to one who can help you.*